NEW FIRST CERTIFICATE ENGLISH
Book 2

Reading
Comprehension

W S Fowler

Thomas Nelson and Sons Ltd
Nelson House   Mayfield Road
Walton-on-Thames   Surrey KT12 5PL

51 York Place
Edinburgh EH1 3JD

Yi Xiu Factory Building
Unit 05-06   5th Floor
65 Sims Avenue   Singapore 1438

Thomas Nelson (Hong Kong) Ltd
Toppan Building 10/F
22A Westlands Road
Quarry Bay   Hong Kong

Thomas Nelson (Kenya) Ltd
P.O. Box 18123
Nairobi   Kenya

First published by Thomas Nelson and Sons Ltd 1984

ISBN 0-17-555525-7

NCN 71 ECE 9162 01

Typeset by H Charlesworth & Co Ltd, Huddersfield

Printed in Great Britain by Butler & Tanner Ltd, Frome and
London

NEW FIRST CERTIFICATE ENGLISH
Book 2

Reading Comprehension

W S Fowler

Nelson

Contents

Introduction

Introduction

● *New First Certificate English*

Since its publication in 1973–5, *First Certificate English* has been the course most widely used by students preparing for the Cambridge examination at this level. In these ten years, however, English teaching methodology has changed considerably, and now the examination itself is to be modified, with effect from June 1984. In preferring to write a new course, which will be published to coincide with the appearance of the new examination, rather than to revise the original, my co-authors, John Pidcock and Robin Rycroft, and I have been primarily concerned to take these changes in methodology into account. Over 90% of the material in the course is new.

While this was in our view a necessary step, it does not mean that the examination as such has changed to a noticeable extent either in level or form. As far as the Reading Comprehension paper is concerned, for example, there is a reduction in the number of lexical items, and instead of two passages for comprehension with ten questions on each, there will now be three passages (one of which will be in the form of a notice or advertisement) with five questions. The main reason for a new book was therefore that after ten years' further experience of teaching Cambridge examination classes, I have modified my own ideas.

● The design of the course

The four books comprising the new course can be used independently in order to concentrate on a specific paper in the examination, but they have been written in such a way that they relate to each other. In so far as this book is concerned, the 24 units parallel the 24 units of *Book 1 Language and Composition*, and develop through passages and exercises an understanding of the themes and lexis contained there. This is not to suggest that they are a repetition. For one thing, whereas my co-author and I wrote almost all of the texts for *Book 1* ourselves, in this case they have almost all been selected from modern British and American authors and are presented without simplification. The relationship is one of theme; the first unit of *Book 1*, for instance, is devoted to descriptions of people, and the first passage in this book compares a publisher's imaginary picture of authors he has never met with the reality, when they actually arrive.

● Lexis and comprehension

As stated above, the Cambridge examination in Reading Comprehension consists of two sections which require related, but, to some extent, different areas of knowledge and technical skills. I have discussed them separately below but it is not my intention to suggest that they should be divided off. The units of the book serve two purposes throughout; they exemplify lexis in context, the only way in which new vocabulary can be satisfactorily learned and subsequently used, and they also serve as passages for comprehension. I have used a wide variety of exercises in this connection, explained in more detail below. These exercises, preceding and following the passages, are presented in the order in which I habitually use them in the classroom.

● Lexis

The meaning of words can only be learnt in context, and students must overcome, if they have not done so already, the habit of asking what words mean and expecting an instant translation, which is likely to be imprecise, before they have attempted to work out the meaning for themselves. If they can do this, as they will be able to in the majority of cases, they will have learnt the meaning in such a way that they are more likely to remember it and less likely to confuse its potential use.

The lexical exercises in this book have three main purposes:

1) to help students to decide on the meaning of new words in context;

2) to expand their vocabulary in general terms by associating words with appropriate contexts and differentiating between them;

3) to point out words that are commonly confused either because they are apparently similar in meaning in English (e.g. **raise**, **rise**), or because they are deceptively close to words with a rather different range of usage in their own language (e.g. **advertise**, **advise**, **announce**, etc.) for speakers of Latin languages.

The second point here is perhaps the most important, not only in the sense of distinguishing, for example, between **house**, **flat** and **cottage**, but also because a large proportion of Cambridge examination items are set phrases, where there is no logical explanation of the choice of words from a foreigner's point of view, e.g. we say a lift is **out of order**, not 'out of function' or 'out of work'.

I have dealt with these problems as follows. In the first case, I have considered whether the meaning of unfamiliar words in the text (i.e. those classified as beyond First Certificate level in the *Cambridge English Lexicon* by Roland Hindmarsh, which is used as the lexical basis for the examination) can reasonably be deduced from the context. If it can be, I have provided students with alternatives from which they should be able to choose the correct definition; if not, or if a cultural item of information is involved, I have given an explanation alongside. Vocabulary expansion is handled in two main ways. First, I have as far as possible introduced the theme of the passage with warm-up exercises, primarily reminding students of words they already know, but also introducing some related words that may be less familiar; secondly, I have asked them to find words in the passage either similar or opposite in meaning to those I have provided in the exercise, thereby confirming

their understanding of them. Here, of course, teachers may need to draw students' attention to differences, since true similes are rare, and advice is offered in the *Teacher's Guide*. In the third case, I have produced model sentences and short paragraphs enabling the students to distinguish clearly between words that are commonly confused.

I have not attempted to exemplify phrasal verbs except where they occur naturally in the passages quoted. I have, however, provided an appendix with definitions of the most commonly used ones and with sentences exemplifying areas of usage.

Apart from the three test papers at the end of the book, there are four lexical tests, appearing at intervals of six units, in which all the items are drawn from the lexis previously presented. These tests have been thoroughly pretested according to the guidelines laid down by Cambridge for the selection of items in their own syllabus and sample paper. I am very grateful for the kind collaboration of the 600 students who took part in the pretesting, which was carried out in two schools in Barcelona where the average annual pass rate for the examination is over 90%. Full details of the pretesting appear in the *Teacher's Guide*.

● **Comprehension**

It has long been my contention (stated in the Introduction to *Proficiency English*, *Book 2*, published in 1977) that multiple-choice questions, whatever their merits as testing instruments elsewhere, are unsuitable for testing comprehension because they give rise to ambiguity and very often test students' logical powers rather than their understanding of language. For this reason, since Cambridge continue to use this testing method, I have endeavoured to provide students with as much help as possible so that they can develop the techniques to deal with it. While I believe teachers should ask direct questions in class in the first instance, I have also included a series of exercises that build up gradually to the multiple-choice formula of four choices used in the examination. In the early units of the book, students are asked direct questions or asked to decide if a statement about the content of the passage is true or false; from Unit 13 onwards, they are usually given three choices, and only in Unit 22 is this increased to four. The delay is deliberate, since what the student needs to develop is the capacity to eliminate wrong answers; a concentration on multiple-choice from the beginning normally results in students being unable to resist looking at the choices before they even read the passage, which is counter-productive in every way.

● Reading

Reading is of vital importance to anyone learning a foreign language. It should be an enjoyable experience, and will be, if the texts are sufficiently interesting in themselves and within the students' range of understanding (which means not that they understand every word but that they can follow the text without having to reach for a dictionary). The passages here are of three kinds. The majority are modern journalism from 'quality' newspapers; there are a number from well-known modern writers; finally, there are some that represent a new departure in the Cambridge examination itself, where one of the three passages chosen will be in the form of a notice or advertisement and students are expected to derive the correct information from it. It is my hope that after studying this book, students will be encouraged to read more widely and be better equipped to do so.

Will Fowler
Barcelona, June 1983

● Acknowledgements

I am very grateful to the teachers and students of the British Council Institute, Barcelona, and to Peter Clements, Director, and the teachers and students of the CIC, Barcelona, for their help in pretesting all the test materials in this book.

Thanks are due to the following for permission to reproduce copyright material:

pp. 5–6, 8, 76–7: *The Sunday Times Magazine* 6.1.80; pp. 10, 12, 67, 69: College Trustees Ltd. for the Estate of Raymond Chandler, and Hamish Hamilton Ltd.; pp. 14, 20: William Collins Sons & Co. Ltd.; pp. 16, 78–9, 85–7: Mrs James Thurber and Hamish Hamilton Ltd. (Copr. © 1957 James Thurber. From *Alarms and Diversions*, published by Harper & Row), (© Hamish Hamilton 1963 taken from *Vintage*

Thurber edited by Helen Thurber); pp. 18–19, 56: *The Observer* (Copyright © *The Observer* Ltd., London); pp. 22, 89: *Telegraph Sunday Magazine*; p. 24: Graham Greene, William Heinemann Ltd. and The Bodley Head Ltd., and Viking Penguin Inc.; pp. 27, 54, 58–9, 61–2, 106: *The Daily Telegraph*; pp. 28–9: Penguin Books Ltd. (Copyright © Ronald Blythe, 1979. Reprinted by permission of Penguin Books Ltd.); p. 33: Josephine Tey and Peter Davies; p. 34: Geoffrey Wheatcroft (Original publication *Sunday Telegraph* © 1983 by Geoffrey Wheatcroft); pp. 39–40: *The Daily Telegraph* Careers Information Service; p. 42: National Westminister Bank PLC; pp. 44–5: Mrs James Thurber and Hamish Hamilton Ltd. (Copr. © 1945 James Thurber. Copr. © 1973 Helen W. Thurber and Rosemary T. Sauers. From *The Thurber Carnival*, published by Harper & Row.), (© Hamish Hamilton 1963 taken from Vintage Thurber edited by Helen Thurber); p. 47: William Bayer and Ridge Press Inc.; pp. 51–2: Mr Irwin Lowen, Senior Vice President, SAI Group; pp. 64–5: The Bodley Head Ltd. and Alfred A. Knopf Inc. (Reprinted by permission of The Bodley Head Ltd. from *The Americans* by Alistair Cooke); p. 81: *Financial Times*; p. 83: Crown copyright. Reproduced with the permission of the Controller of Her Majesty's Stationery Office; pp. 91–2, 96: Christopher Hibbert, J. B. Lippincott Company and Harper & Row Publ. Inc.; p. 97: *The Sunday Times Magazine* 11.1.81 for an extract from 'Message to Shoplifters: Don't smile, you're on television' by Russell Miller; p. 98: Labour Research Department; pp. 101, 102: *The Guardian* for extracts from 'Missing' by Barbara Lamb, and from 'Spending on school computer lessons doubled'; p. 103: The Health Education Council for an extract from their booklet *So You Want to Stop Smoking*; p. 105: *Telegraph Sunday Magazine* for an extract from 'Around the World in an Orange Balloon' by Jean Rafferty; p. 106: *The Daily Telegraph* for an extract from an article by John Izbicki from the Education column; p. 107: Automobile Association for an extract from their leaflet *Essential Information for Motoring Abroad*.

Thanks are due to the following for permission to reproduce photographs:

Weld Dixon International Ltd. p. 18   National Film Archive/London Films/EMI p. 24   John Shepperson p. 29   Keystone Press pp. 39, 50   National Westminster Bank PLC p. 41   National Film Archive/RKO/Harris p. 47   Format p. 58   Syndication International p. 73   BBC Hulton Picture Library pp. 89, 91.

Every effort has been made to trace owners of copyright and if any omissions can be rectified the publishers will be pleased to make the necessary arrangements.

People

Introductory exercise

*Before looking at the passage below, answer
these questions.*

1 Would a man or woman be more likely to
wear: **a** a collar and tie; **b** a skirt; **c** a blouse;
d a waistcoat; **e** stockings; **f** a dress?

2 Would they wear these items of clothing
mainly above or below the waist? Or half and
half?

3 Would the following be worn: **a** round the
waist; **b** round the neck; **c** round the ankles;
d in the hair?
a scarf, a collar, a belt, a ribbon, bicycle clips.

4 Point to your jaw, chin, lips, cheeks, forehead,
throat, shoulders, knees, wrists, ankles.

The unexpected brothers

Over a hundred years ago, a publisher was waiting in his
London office for three brothers to arrive. They had sent him
some poems, and he was looking forward to meeting them,
especially the second brother, Ellis Bell, who obviously had the
5 most talent. At first he had thought of sending someone to meet
their train from Yorkshire, but he had no idea what they looked
like.

While he was waiting, he looked out of the window. A cab
drew up outside and two ladies got out. They wore black
10 bonnets, tied tightly round their necks with ribbons, and long,
rather shabby dresses; they were obviously respectable, but not
well off. One of them paid the driver while the other looked
around her timorously, as if she was unfamiliar with the streets
of a big city, and the surroundings frightened her.

15 The publisher returned to his desk and amused himself by
trying to form an impression of the brothers from their poems.
Currer Bell was probably the eldest, no doubt a serious
clergyman, with long side-whiskers framing his face, but a
romantic at heart; Acton seemed less experienced, perhaps a
20 sweet-natured young man who hoped to marry a girl but was
too shy to tell her so. The third, Ellis, must be quite different.
The publisher imagined him to be tall, with long, black hair
streaming in the wind behind him as he strode across the
moors, reciting his poems to himself.

25 The door opened. His secretary announced the arrival of two
visitors. 'There are two ladies here, sir,' he said. 'They say they
have an appointment.' The publisher looked up in amazement.

'I'm expecting three gentlemen to call,' he said, 'but no ladies.'
At that moment a diminutive woman – she could not have been
30 five feet tall – with a plain, round, but determined face,
appeared in the doorway. 'I am Currer Bell,' she said. 'Ah,' said
the publisher, 'and this,' he added, indicating the girl beside
her, and guessing correctly, 'must be Acton.' 'Yes,' said Currer
Bell, whose real name was **Charlotte Brontë**. 'We could not
35 persuade Ellis – that is, my sister Emily – to accompany us.'

Charlotte Brontë: (1816–55), author of *Jane Eyre*, was the elder sister of Emily (1818–48), who wrote *Wuthering Heights*, and Anne (1820–49), who also published novels.

Guessing the meaning of a word from the context

Before trying to find the meaning of a word in a dictionary, always try to guess it from the context. There are ways in which you can help your guesses. First, what sort of word is it? What part does it play in the phrases or sentence?

Look at these examples.
1 ... as he **strode** *across the moors.* (line 23) **Strode** must be a verb, and it is in the Past tense, because the previous verb is **imagined**. Cover the word over in the passage and you will see that it must be a verb in the Past tense.
2 *They wore black **bonnets***. (line 10) **Bonnets** must be a noun in plural form.
3 ... *a **diminutive** woman ... appeared.* (line 29) **Diminutive** must be an adjective because of its position before the noun, **woman**.
4 ... *the other looked around her **timorously***. (line 13) **Timorously** tells us how she looked, so it must be an adverb.
5 ... *he had thought of sending someone **to meet** their train.* (line 5) The form tells us that this is an infinitive.
6 ... *he was looking forward **to meeting** them.* (line 3) But here the form tells us that **to**, followed by a gerund, is not part of an infinitive, but a preposition.
7 *The third, Ellis, **must** be quite different.* (line 21) The main verb is **be**, which cannot stand alone in this form, so **must**, of course, is an auxiliary.

Many unfamiliar words can be guessed from the context, once you have decided what sort of

word they are. **Unfamiliar** itself, which appears in the previous sentence and also in the passage clearly has nothing to do with families. It describes something you are not accustomed to, or do not recognise immediately.

Now look at the first four quotations once again.
1 **strode:** a verb, suggesting movement. 'Walked', rather than 'ran', because people don't recite poems when they are running. How do you suppose this imaginary character would walk? (It means 'walked with long steps'.)
2 The ladies were wearing **bonnets**. Where? They were tied round their necks. And this took place over a hundred years ago. A bonnet is a hat, usually tied under the chin, worn by women, although not nowadays.
3 **diminutive:** Well, she was under five feet tall (1.52 metres). Very small!
4 **timorously:** 'as if ... the surroundings frightened her.' So ...?

Exercise 1

Using the same technique, decide from the context a) what sort of words the following are and b) what they probably mean. Even if you know the words already, explain why the context indicates the correct choice from the clues given.
1 **cab** (line 8): the nineteenth-century equivalent of *a* a bus? *b* a taxi?
2 **drew up** (line 9): *a* started? *b* stopped?

3 **shabby** (line 11): describes their dresses. The ladies were not well off.
4 **side whiskers** (line 18): at the side of what? A hundred years ago, many men wore beards, but these do not make a beard.
5 **framing** (line 18): **a** covering? **b** giving shape to?
6 **streaming** (line 23): like water, flowing? Yes, but as a result of what? What idea is being expressed here?
7 **reciting** (line 24): saying, clearly. But what was he saying?

Synonyms — Exercise 2

One way of expanding your vocabulary is to think of words that mean almost the same as the words used in the context, though you must remember that there are very few synonyms in English, and the writer presumably preferred the word he/she chose for a reason.

Find words or phrases in the passage that are similar in meaning to the following. The number in brackets indicates the paragraph where the word or phrase is to be found.
1 clearly (2)
2 rich (2)
3 not used to (2)
4 went back (3)
5 attempting (3)
6 totally (3)
7 surprise (4)
8 entrance (4)
9 come with (4)

Vocabulary expansion — Exercise 3

Another way of expanding vocabulary is to consider that we use different words for similar things.
e.g. If the sisters had come by bus (if buses had existed!), the publisher might have sent someone to meet them at the **bus station** or the **bus stop**, not the station.
1 Nowadays, they might have come by plane, and he would have sent someone to the

_____

2 The ladies wore dresses, but if they had really been three brothers, they would have worn
_____.
3 They arrived over a hundred years ago in a cab, but if they arrived nowadays, they would take a _____.

Words often confused — Exercise 4

A major problem in reading in a foreign language is to avoid confusing words similar in meaning but different in structure and usage, especially those that may look like words in your own language.

● **A   expect, hope, look forward to, wait (for)**

Study the way in which these words are used in the passage as you answer the following questions.
1 Did the publisher expect two ladies to call?
2 Who did he expect to see? What did he expect them to look like?
3 Why did he look forward to meeting Ellis more than the others?
4 Why was he waiting in his office? Who was he waiting for?
5 Why (in his imagination) didn't Acton speak to the girl he hoped to marry? Why didn't he expect to marry her? In what circumstances would he look forward to marrying her?

● **B   find, get to know, know, meet**

*Use each verb, **at least once**, in the correct form to complete the following.*
I first ¹_____ Colin over twenty years ago at the university, and ²_____ him very well over the next two years. When he emigrated to Canada, I kept in touch with him and always looked forward to ³_____ him again. Last month he wrote to say he was coming to England so I agreed to ⁴_____ at the airport. I waited for him for a long time but couldn't see him so I went into the customs hall to ⁵_____ him. Of course I thought I ⁶_____ him well, but I hadn't seen him for twenty years. Then a bald-headed, middle-aged man came up to me and said: 'Excuse me, are you David Stafford?' I ⁷_____ who he was as soon as he spoke. Fortunately, his voice had not changed.

● **C   advertise, announce, advise, notice**

*Use each verb, **at least once**, in the correct form to complete the following.*

1   The secretary _____ that there were two ladies to see him. 'There are two ladies outside,' he said.
2   When he looked out of the window, he _____ two ladies getting out of a cab.
3   They couldn't find a flat that suited them so I _____ them to _____ in the local newspaper.
4   The headmaster _____ to all the boys that he had _____ that some of them came to school untidily dressed, and _____ them to dress more smartly in future.

Places

Introductory exercise

*Before looking at the passage below, answer
these questions.*

1 In which room of the house would you expect
to find: *a* a sink; *b* a washbasin;
c a wardrobe; *d* a cocktail cabinet; *e* a chest
of drawers; *f* a dressing table; *g* a shower;
h a washing machine?

2 What are the following usually made of?
(More than one answer may be possible.)
a roofs; *b* floors; *c* ceilings; *d* the outside
walls; *e* windows; *f* window frames.

A house in the Hérault

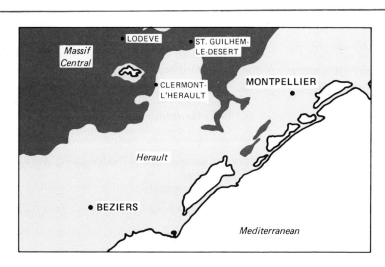

The first time I came to the
Hérault, after a ten-hour train ride
from Paris to Montpellier, I caught a
bus to the old village where my friend
5 Sarah had bought a house. When I got
there an hour and a half later, despite
the fact that I'd been riding on a
twentieth-century bus, I had the
dreamy, disoriented sense that I'd
10 stepped back 700 years.

Sarah's house is made of stone, a
few hundred years old, typical of the
kind of place for sale cheaply here.
Like virtually all the village houses
15 it's attached to the neighbouring ones

– so although the village is small it
feels densely populated, everybody
living close together, always
somebody leaning out of the window
20 or sitting in front of the door. Inside,
it is dark and cool. When Sarah
bought the house, it had cold running
water, some missing floors, a
fireplace that didn't work,
25 treacherous old-fashioned wiring.

To restore a house in the Hérault,
to retrieve its original form, the basic
method is to take damaged structures
apart, noting the sequence in which
30 they were put together. Then, each

part is replaced in turn with sound materials, abundantly available both from the land itself and from the local people, who are dismantling their
35 own houses and 'modernising' them (of course).

To repair her fireplace, Sarah and two friends first spent a week collecting red sandstone from stream
40 beds and fields, over an area of about two square miles. All building is done with rough, uncut stone, so the material can be used as found. The fireplace was built around a wooden
45 mould carved by a young French sculptor. A copper hood was fixed over the hearth to diffuse heat. The back and base of the hearth are cast-iron plates, recovered from the
50 abandoned communal village baker's oven.

The sink came from a **nunnery** and cost £1. On a village dump, she found a beautiful old oval mirror, only
55 slightly chipped, and some odd, diamond-shaped tiles in various shades of blue to frame it. Most of her furniture was recovered from the dumps – also the greater part of her
60 kitchen utensils and appliances, including an old gas stove and two beautiful enamel wood-burning stoves. Dumping is not just for the destitute; all kinds of people
65 take advantage of it. It's more like hunting for antiques – especially popular with the French on Sundays. One couple waited two years until they had collected enough perfect
70 **terra cotta** tiles to make a floor for their living room.

nunnery: convent, house where nuns live

terra cotta: hard, reddish-brown pottery

From *Life in the World's Largest Vineyard* by Maxine Feifer in the *Sunday Times Magazine*

Exercise 1

Decide from the context what sort of words the following are. Choose the most likely meaning of these words in the context of the passage.
1 **disoriented** (line 9): *a* western *b* confused
2 **treacherous** (line 25): *a* weak *b* unreliable
3 **sequence** (line 29): *a* order *b* way
4 **dismantling** (line 34): *a* rebuilding *b* taking apart
5 **the destitute** (line 64): *a* the rich *b* the very poor

Exercise 2

Words often have more than one meaning; the context should tell you if the most familiar meaning is obviously not intended.
e.g. Stream **beds** are not places where people sleep, but the ground over which streams (little rivers) run, perhaps dry in summer.

Decide what the following familiar words mean in the context of the passage.
1 sound (line 31)
2 plates (line 49)
3 shades (line 57)
4 hunting (line 66)

Exercise 3

In many cases, the context indicates the kind of thing the word means.
e.g. 'Somebody **leaning** out of a window' suggests an action with the top half of the body forward, outside the window, but the feet and legs in the room inside.

Work out a definition of the following words in the same way.
1 copper (line 46)
2 hearth (line 47)
3 oven (line 51)
4 dump (line 53)
5 utensils (line 60)
6 stove (line 61)
7 antiques (line 66)

Exercise 4

One way of finding out if you understand a passage is to ask yourself true/false questions about it. The correct answers in multiple-choice questions are often the original words phrased differently.

*Decide whether the following statements are true or false **and** (very important) find a phrase or sentence in the passage justifying your decision.*

e.g. The writer arrived at the village by train.
      (False: 'I caught a bus to the old village'.)

1   When Sarah bought the house it had no heating.
2   One of the risks in the house was that she might get an electric shock.
3   If part of the house is damaged, the usual method in the Hérault is to knock it all down and replace it with something new.
4   The fireplace Sarah built was made of wood.
5   Sarah bought the back and base of the hearth from a baker.
6   French people despise those like Sarah who collect furniture from dumps.

Exercise 5

● **A**

Find words or phrases in the passage that are similar in meaning to the following. The number in brackets indicates the paragraph where the word or phrase is to be found.

1   in spite of (1)
2   almost (2)
3   one after another (3)

● **B**

Find adjectives that mean the opposite of the following, in the context of the passage.

1   large (2)
2   light (2)
3   warm (2)
4   hot (2)
5   smooth (4)

Exercise 6

● **A** **flat, floor, ground, level, stage**

Choose the correct word to complete the following. Use plural forms where appropriate.

1   Before moving to the South of France Sarah lived in a _____ in Paris. The _____ was on the seventh _____.
2   He picked up the cigarette packet from the _____ and threw it out of the window. It fell on the _____ outside.
3   The _____ of the theatre where the actors perform is called the _____.
4   The first _____ in restoring a house is to take damaged structures apart. In Sarah's case, some _____ were missing, so when she replaced them, it raised the _____.

● **B** **damaged, hurt, wounded**

Choose the correct word to complete the following.

Some of the soldiers were ¹_____ in the battle, and when the hospital was bombed afterwards, other patients were ²_____ and the hospital itself was badly ³_____.

● **C** **couple, pair, set**

Look at the use of these words in the following phrases and decide when each word can be used.

e.g. a married **couple**
      a **pair** of shoes
      a chess **set**
      a couple of dogs and a cat

Choose the correct word to complete the following.

1   We were dancing next to another _____.
2   I've bought three _____ of socks.
3   We've given him a _____ of tools for his workshop as a birthday present.
4   I've seen her a _____ of times over the last few weeks.

Holiday in Portugal

If the only experience of Portugal you have is of **the Algarve**, dry and dusty in August, you will be unprepared for the lush greenness of the North. In mid-
5 June the roadsides were a mass of flowers in bloom.

Our base for the first few days of our tour was Povoa de Varzim, half an hour's drive north of Oporto, where you
10 can amuse yourself in the casino or just enjoy the Atlantic. There are modern hotels right on the beach, which is vast, sandy and clean but beset by wind for much of the summer. The tourist
15 season gets under way about mid-July, but it is warm long before, and early holidays can be rewarding.

The Costa Verde, like its hinterland the Minho, is a land of terraced
20 hillsides, pine and eucalyptus forests and empty, winding roads (the surface of which may be a bit daunting: chiefly cobblestones). There are more barefoot women carrying bundles on
25 their heads than wheeled vehicles — and even these tend to be bullock carts rather than motor cars. It is not the easiest place to take a caravan.

One of our excursions was to
30 Barcelos, 15 miles east of Povoa. It has a busy open-air market — really interesting, not just tourist junk.

In Oporto itself, a beautiful city of steep, narrow streets and tall buildings,
35 it is **de rigueur** to visit the wine lodges along **the Douro** where much of the world's port is made and stored: generous tastings of the various types are organised. Food in Portugal is not
40 particularly light, but the seafood is in general splendid.

the Algarve: an area in the south of Portugal
de rigueur: socially obligatory
the Douro: the river at Oporto

From *Spain and Portugal: the north-west* by Gilvrie Misstear in the *Sunday Times Magazine*

Exercise 1

Choose the most likely meaning of these words or phrases in the context of the passage. If in doubt, ask yourself the questions in brackets before deciding.

1 **lush** (line 3): *a* rocky *b* growing luxuriantly (UNprepared?)
2 **beset** (line 13): *a* troubled *b* destroyed (By wind?)
3 **gets under way** (line 15): *a* starts *b* ends (In mid-July?)
4 **hinterland** (line 18): *a* the land on the coast *b* the land behind the coast
5 **winding** (line 21): *a* straight *b* with bends (On a hillside?)
6 **daunting** (line 22): *a* hard *b* discouraging (*May* be ...)
7 **junk** (line 32): *a* rubbish *b* equipment (Interesting, not just ...)

Exercise 2

Find phrases or sentences in the passage to show whether these statements are true or false, and use them to justify your answer.

1 The writer travelled around Portugal by car.
2 It is unwise to visit Povoa de Varzim before July.
3 Most people on the Costa Verde get about by bullock cart.
4 The market at Barcelos only has souvenirs.
5 The writer is not fond of Portuguese food.

Exercise 3

Look at the example given before answering the questions below.

e.g. A *sandy* beach means that the surface is formed of sand.

1   What is the surface formed of if we say:
    a dusty; *b* grassy; *c* muddy; *d* rocky; *e* stony?
2   On which of these could you walk barefoot?
3   In which cases would you probably have to clean your shoes afterwards?

Exercise 4

● A   bank, beach, coast, harbour, port

Choose the correct word, either in singular or plural form, to complete the following.

The ^{1}_____ on the ^{2}_____ north of Oporto are sandy. Oporto, as its name suggests, is a ^{3}_____, with a ^{4}_____ to shelter ships. Along the ^{5}_____ of the Douro you can drink the other kind of port, which the area is famous for.

● B   amuse (oneself), enjoy (oneself), entertain

Use each verb **twice**, the first two reflexively on one occasion, to complete the following.

He ^{1}_____ ten guests to dinner last night. He ^{2}_____ (2 possibilities) them by telling funny stories. I ^{3}_____ myself very much at the dinner. I ^{4}_____ the company and the food. But Hector was bored. He ^{5}_____ himself by making paper aeroplanes.

● C   period, season, term, time

Choose the correct word to complete each of the following expressions.

1   the holiday _____
2   the school _____
3   a long _____ of time
4   a _____ of imprisonment
5   lunch _____
6   in the mediaeval _____
7   the football _____

Interviews

Introductory exercise

*Before looking at the passage below, answer
these questions.*

1 When do people usually: *a* smile; *b* laugh;
c stare; *d* blush; *e* tremble; *f* grin; *g* frown;
h shiver?

2 When do they: *a* shake hands; *b* shake their
heads; *c* nod; *d* scratch their heads; *e* bite
their lips?

Before the interview

It was a small room looking out on the back garden. It had an ugly
red and brown carpet and was furnished as an office. It contained
what you would expect to find in a small office. A thin, fragile-
looking, blondish girl in shell glasses sat behind a desk with a
5 typewriter on a pulled-out leaf at her left. She had her hands poised
on the keys, but she didn't have any paper in the machine. She
watched me come into the room with the stiff, half-silly expression
of a self-conscious person posing for a snapshot. She had a clear,
soft voice, asking me to sit down.
10 'I am Miss Davis. Mrs Murdock's secretary. She wanted me to
ask you for a few references.'
'References?'
'Certainly. References. Does that surprise you?'
I put my hat on her desk and the unlighted cigarette on the brim of
15 the hat. 'You mean she sent for me without knowing anything about
me?'
Her lip trembled and she bit it. I didn't know whether she was
scared or annoyed or just having trouble being cool and business-
like. But she didn't look happy.
20 'She got your name from the manager of a branch of the
California-Security Bank. But he doesn't know you personally,' she
said.
'Get your pencil ready,' I said.
She held it up and showed me that it was freshly sharpened and
25 ready to go.
I gave her a few names and addresses. She wrote fast and easily.
She nodded without looking up. The light danced on her blonde
hair.
'Don't laugh at me,' she said 'I'm only doing what I'm told.'

From *The High Window* by Raymond Chandler (abridged)

Exercise 1

Choose the most likely meaning of these words in the context of the passage.
1 **poised** (line 5): *a* heavy *b* ready
2 **self-conscious** (line 8): *a* aware of people watching *b* proud of oneself
3 **posing** (line 8): *a* pretending *b* taking up a position
4 **brim** (line 14): *a* the out-turned part of the hat *b* the inside of a hat

Exercise 2

Decide from the context what sort of thing is meant by these familiar words.
1 shell (line 4)
2 leaf (line 5)
3 keys (line 6)
4 danced (line 27)

Exercise 3

● A

Find words or phrases in the passage that are similar in meaning to the following. The number in brackets indicates the paragraph where the word or phrase is to be found.
1 photograph (1)
2 frightened (6)
3 irritated (6)
4 calm (6)
5 efficient (6)

● B

Find words that mean the opposite of the following, in the context of the passage.
1 beautiful (1)
2 relaxed (1)
3 slowly (10)
4 with difficulty (10)
5 dark (10)

Exercise 4

Find three adjectives in the first paragraph that suggest the girl was not entirely what she seemed. Note the way in which these adjectives are formed.

Exercise 5

● A   look at, notice, stare (at), watch

Read the following sentences and then put the verbs in order of increasing intensity.
1 She **watched** me come into the room.
2 She looked up from the typewriter and **noticed** me.
3 She **stared at** me for a long time.
4 She **looked at** me self-consciously.

● B   appearance, expression, look, sight, view

Answer these questions and decide how these words are used.
1 Describe the girl's **appearance**, as far as you can.
2 What sort of **expression** did she have on her face when the narrator came in? Was she smiling?
3 Do you think she wrote down the names and addresses with a **look** of interest?
4 Was the room an interesting **sight**?
5 What was the **view** from the room?

● C   anxiety, nuisance, problem, trouble

Choose the correct word to complete the following. Each word appears at least once. Which words are uncountable nouns in the context?
There was some cause for ¹_____ in the girl's behaviour, but I wasn't sure if she was just having ²_____ trying to look efficient. It was rather a ³_____ having to give references. I thought Mrs Murdock would have taken the ⁴_____ to find out who I was before she sent for me, but it wasn't a serious ⁵_____.

The interview itself

A short time after talking to the secretary,
Marlowe was taken to see Mrs Murdock.

I stood there. She let me stand while she finished the port in her glass
and put the glass down on the table and filled it again. Then she
tapped her lips with a handkerchief. Then she spoke. Her voice
had a hard baritone quality and sounded as if it didn't want any
5 nonsense.

'Sit down, Mr Marlowe. Please do not light that cigarette. I'm
asthmatic.'

I sat down and tucked the still unlighted cigarette down behind
the handkerchief in my outside pocket.

10 'I've never had any dealing with private detectives, Mr Marlowe.
I don't know anything about them. Your references seem
satisfactory. What are your charges?'

'To do what, Mrs Murdock?'

'It's a very confidential matter, naturally. Nothing to do with the
15 police. If it had to do with the police I should have called the police.'

'I charge twenty-five dollars a day, Mrs Murdock. And, of course,
expenses.'

'It seems high. You must make a great deal of money.' She drank
some more of her port. I don't like port in hot weather, but it's nice
20 when they let you refuse it.

'No,' I said. 'It isn't. Of course, you can get detective work done
at any price – just like legal work. Or dental work. I'm not an
organisation. I'm just one man and I work at just one case at a time. I
take risks, sometimes quite big risks, and I don't work all the time.
25 No, I don't think twenty- five dollars a day is too much.'

'I see. And what is the nature of the expenses?'

'Little things that come up here and there. You never know.'

'I should prefer to know,' she said acidly.

'You'll know,' I said. 'You'll get it all down in black and white.
30 You'll have a chance to object if you don't like it.'

From *The High Window*
by Raymond Chandler

Exercise 1

After reading the passage, answer these
questions. Check the meaning of any words
you do not know.
1   What is strange about Mrs Murdock having a
    baritone voice?
2   How do you know, from the passage, that
    asthmatic people are allergic to smoke?
3   Find a common verb to replace **tucked**.
4   What indicates that the case is **confidential**?
5   What do you think is the origin of the phrase
    in black and white?

Exercise 2

Understanding a passage is not always a
question of recognising facts that are stated,
but sometimes of feeling the atmosphere.
Find: a) two actions that show Mrs Murdock
was rude; b) two phrases suggesting she was
mean with money; c) two phrases that show
she was used to speaking directly.

Exercise 3

Say whether these statements are true or false, and justify your answer.
1   Marlowe sat down and lit a cigarette.
2   Mrs Murdock had already decided he was unsuitable for the case.
3   Marlowe didn't object to her rudeness.
4   Marlowe didn't agree that his charges were high.
5   Mrs Murdock agreed to pay his expenses without question.

Exercise 4

● A   charge, cost, pay, spend

Use each verb once only in the correct form to complete the following.
Marlowe ¹_____ 25 dollars a day. Mrs Murdock thinks his services ²_____ a great deal and isn't sure she will ³_____ him so much. She is not the sort of woman who likes ⁴_____ money on anything.

● B   charge, price, prize, reward

Choose the correct word, in either the singular or plural form, to complete the following.
Marlowe makes a ¹_____ for his services. If he were a shopkeeper, Mrs Murdock would want to know the ²_____ of the goods. If he catches a murderer, the police might give him a ³_____, but detectives seldom win ⁴_____.

● C

Explain where and when you would pay the following.
1   a bill
2   rent
3   fees
4   duty
5   a fine
6   taxes
7   a debt
8   expenses
9   an allowance
10 a fare

● D   a great deal of, a large number of, a considerable amount of

Which of the other two phrases above could replace **a great deal of** in the phrase 'a great deal of money' (line 18) in the passage?

● E   deny (doing), object (to ... doing), refuse (to do), reject

Use one of these verbs to describe each of the following statements.
1   'No thank you. I don't like port in hot weather.'
2   'I don't think you should include drinks in your expenses.'
3   'I don't think your references are good enough for this job.'
4   'I'm not going to take the case.'
5   'I didn't commit any crime.'

Family life

4

Introductory exercise

Before looking at the passage below, answer these questions.

What subjects would you study if you wanted to be: *a* a doctor; *b* a biologist; *c* an author; *d* a translator; *e* an astronomer; *f* a historian; *g* an engineer; *h* a lawyer; *i* a clergyman; *j* an explorer?

Inviting a friend

George introduced me to someone who was immediately to become the most important person in my life: Dr Theodore Stephanides. To me, Theodore was one of the most remarkable people I had ever met (and thirty-three years later I am still of the
5 same opinion). With his ash-blond hair and beard and his handsome **aquiline** features, he looked like a Greek god, and certainly he seemed as omniscient as one. Apart from being medically qualified, he was also a biologist, a poet, author, translator, astronomer and historian and he found time between
10 those multifarious activities to help to run an X-ray laboratory, the only one of its kind, in the town of Corfu. After my first visit to his flat in town, I asked Mother **tentatively** whether I might ask him to come to tea with us.
   'I suppose so, dear,' said Mother. 'I hope he speaks English,
15 though.'
   I said indignantly that Theodore could speak excellent English: in fact, if anything, better English than we could. Soothed by this, Mother suggested that I write Theodore a note and invite him out for the following Thursday. I spent an
20 agonised two hours hanging about the garden waiting for him to arrive, peering every few minutes through the fuchsia hedge, a prey to the most terrible emotions. Perhaps the note had never reached him? Or perhaps he had put it in his pocket and forgotten about it and was, at this moment, **gallivanting**
25 **eruditely** at the southernmost tip of the island? Or perhaps he had heard about the family and just didn't want to come? If that was the case, I vowed, I would not lightly forgive them. But presently I saw him, neatly tweed-suited, his Homburg squarely on his head, striding up through the olive trees,
30 swinging his stick and humming to himself. Hung over his shoulder was his **collecting bag**, which was as much a part of him as his arms and legs.

aquiline: curved like an eagle's beak

tentatively: as a trial, to see her reaction

gallivanting eruditely: wandering in a learned manner

collecting bag: Theodore collected specimens of insects, plants, etc.

From Birds, Beasts and Relatives by Gerald Durrell

Exercise 1

You can often deduce the meaning of a word from a context by deciding what action, etc. it is likely to be, and then guessing from the word or surrounding information more precisely.

First decide whether each word below suggests a) or b) and then imagine its real meaning.
1 **ash-blond** (line 5): *a* a colour *b* a style (Like what?)
2 **peering** (line 21): an action of *a* moving *b* looking (How?)
3 **fuchsia** (line 21): *a* a plant *b* a material (Why?)
4 **southernmost** (line 25): *a* a height *b* a direction
5 **tweed** (line 28): *a* a material *b* a plant (Why?)
6 **striding** (line 29): an action of *a* making a noise *b* walking
7 **swinging** (line 30): an action involving *a* movement *b* no movement
8 **humming** (line 30): an action involving *a* walking *b* making a noise

Exercise 2

Say whether these statements are true or false, and justify your answer.
1 The narrator has changed his mind about Theodore since he met him.
2 Theodore was the only medically qualified man on the island.
3 If Theodore hadn't wanted to come, the boy would have blamed him.
4 Theodore was smartly dressed when he arrived.
5 He seemed to be sad as he walked along.

Exercise 3

Find words or phrases in the passage that are similar in meaning to the following. The number in brackets indicates the paragraph where the word or phrase is to be found.

1 knowing everything (1)
2 widely different (1)
3 angrily and taking offence (3)
4 comforted (3)
5 very anxious (3)
6 victim of (3)
7 promised (3)
8 firmly (3)

Exercise 4

● A   **become, develop, get, grow, grow up**

In this example the three verbs can all be used with the same meaning, but not in the following exercise.

e.g. He **became/grew/got** old (tired, impatient, etc.).

*Use each verb once, and **two of the verbs twice**, in the correct form to complete the following.*
1 Theodore was to _____ the most important person in his life.
2 When the boy _____ he still admired him.
3 He carried his collecting bag to _____ specimens.
4 Theodore and the boy _____ a firm friendship.
   They _____ firm friends.
5 Fuchsias _____ in Corfu.
6 He _____ all kinds of plants in his garden.

● B   **belief, idea, mind, opinion, view**

In the examples some of these words can be used with the same meaning, but not in the following exercise.

e.g. I am still of the same **opinion/belief/mind**.
      I still have the same **belief/idea/opinion/view**.

Choose the correct word to complete the following.
When the ¹_____ of inviting Theodore came into his ²_____, he asked his mother if it would be all right. In the ³_____ that Theodore could not speak English, she was doubtful, but he told her that in his ⁴_____ (2 possibilities) Theodore spoke English better than the family.

● C advice, letter, message, note, notice

Choose the correct word to complete the following.

1 He put up a _____ outside his home, advertising it for sale.
2 Thanks for ringing. She's out, but I can take a _____, and tell her when she comes in.
3 He wrote Theodore a _____. There was no need for a formal _____.
4 Theodore gave the boy good _____ about birds and insects.

● D actually, at present, presently, recently/lately

Choose the correct word to complete the following.

1 He often came here last year, but I haven't seen him _____. _____, I think he's moved out of the district.
2 There's no one at home _____, but I expect Mary will be back _____.

Husband and wife

RULE FIVE: When a husband is reading aloud, a wife should sit quietly in her chair, relaxed but attentive. She should not keep swinging one foot, start to wind her wristwatch, file her fingernails, or clap her hands in an effort to catch a mosquito.
5 The good wife allows the mosquito to bite her when her husband is reading aloud.
   She should not break in to correct her husband's pronunciation, or to tell him one of his socks is wrong side out. When the husband has finished, the wife should not lunge
10 instantly into some irrelevant subject. It's wiser to exclaim, 'How interesting!' or, at the very least, 'Well, well!' If he should ask some shrewd question to test her attention, she can cry, 'Good heavens!' leap up, and rush out to the kitchen on some urgent fictitious errand. This may fool him, or it may not. I hope, for her
15 sake – and his – that it does.

RULE SEVEN: If a husband is not listening to what his wife is saying, he should not grunt, 'Okay' or 'Yeah, sure,' or make little affirmative noises. A husband lost in thought or worry is likely not to take in the sense of such a statement as this: 'We're going to
20 the Gordons' for dinner tonight, John, so I'm letting the servants off. Don't come home from the office first. Remember, we both have to be at the dentist's at five, and I'll pick you up there with the car.' Now, an 'Okay' or 'Yeah, sure' at this point can raise havoc if the husband hasn't really been listening. As usual, he
25 goes all the way out to his home in Glenville – thirteen miles from the dentist's office and seventeen miles from the Gordons' house – and he can't find his wife. He can't find the servants. His wife can't get him on the phone because all she gets is the busy buzz. John is calling everybody he can think of except, of course, the
30 dentist and the Gordons. At last he hangs up, exhausted and enraged. Then the phone rings. It is his wife. And here let us leave them.

From *Alarms and Diversions* by James Thurber (abridged)

Exercise 1

These are two of ten rules. What do you think they are rules for?

Exercise 2

● A

Choose the most likely meaning of these words or phrases in the context of the passage.
1   **wind** (line 3): involves *a* blowing *b* turning (For what purpose?)
2   **file** (line 3): suggests *a* biting *b* cutting (How?)
3   **clap** (line 4): suggests *a* hitting together *b* holding firmly
4   **lunge into** (lines 9–10): suggests *a* suddenly beginning *b* suddenly ending
5   **leap up** (line 13): suggests *a* sitting up *b* getting up (How quickly?)
6   **rush out** (line 13): suggests *a* going out *b* calling out (Quickly or not?)

● B

1   **Exclaim** (line 10), **cry** (line 12) and **grunt** (line 17) all mean 'say', but in different ways. Decide on the differences from the words spoken.
2   When do we: *a* **shout**; *b* **whisper**?

Exercise 3

Humorous writing depends a great deal on making us imagine a picture — for example, the wife doing what she should not do when her husband is reading — and saying absurd things seriously.

Answer these questions on the passage.
1   Which sentence in the first paragraph does the writer obviously not expect wives to take seriously?
2   What should a wife do to pretend that she has been listening, and how do we know that she has not?
3   Why does the author add: — *and his* — (line 15)?
4   Why is a worried husband likely to make the mistake described in Rule Seven? There are two reasons.
5   Why does the author say: *And here let us leave them* (lines 31–2)?

Exercise 4

Phrasal verbs often have different meanings and only the context tells you which one is intended.

Choose the most likely meaning of these two-part verbs in the context of the passage.
1   **break in** (line 7): *a* interrupt *b* enter a house illegally
2   **take in** (line 19): *a* deceive *b* understand
3   **pick up** (line 22): *a* lift *b* collect
4   **think of** (line 29): *a* imagine *b* remember
5   **hang up** (line 30): *a* put the phone down *b* fix on the wall

Exercise 5

Wrong side out and **the busy buzz** are American English. Do you know what we say for these expressions in British English?

Narrow escapes

Introductory exercise

Before looking at the passage below, answer these questions.

1 What sort of disasters can you insure yourself against? What do you insure a house against? Or a car?
2 Aircraft use high-quality petrol as fuel. What sort of fuel can you use to: **a** make a fire; **b** drive a car; **c** cook food; **d** heat the house?
3 A *pilot pilots* an aircraft. Make similar sentences for: **a** a car; **b** a ship; **c** a bicycle; **d** a racehorse; **e** a horse and cart.
4 *The starboard* is the right-hand side of an aircraft. What do we call the left-hand side?
5 Name as many parts of an aircraft as you can.

An air crash avoided

YOUNG OBSERVER YOUNG OBSERVER

excessive weight: The aircraft was heavier because it had hardly used any fuel.

Only minutes after taking off from London's Heathrow Airport one winter's evening, the pilot of a Boeing 747 saw to his
5 horror that the number four (outer starboard) engine was on fire. The Jumbo, carrying 404 passengers and 14 crew, was bound for Calgary in Canada, and
10 the consequences of fire in an aircraft loaded with fuel for a 5,000-mile trip could have been disastrous.

The Jumbo's pilot, a veteran of
15 the Second World War, calmly informed the air traffic control centre at West Drayton of his plight and declared his intention of returning to Heathrow.
20 When he was first notified of the emergency, the air traffic controller Peter Bish was working the number one north radar position in the dimly lit approach
25 control room of the airport's control tower. It was just after 5.25pm and snow was gusting in from the east.

The pilot told Bish that the fire
30 warning light was still on in the cockpit and he wanted to get down as quickly as possible.

There were no histrionics in the control tower. Bish, who has been
35 at Heathrow since 1971, called his supervisor to say that he had a damaged aircraft returning, and the supervisor signalled a full emergency. This brought airport
40 fire appliances and ambulances racing from their posts to the runway apron, and summoned local brigades to rendezvous points around Heathrow.
45 By the time Bish picked up the Jumbo on his radar screen, it was about five miles north-east of the airfield and had about 15 miles to travel until it could land safely
50 back on the runway it had left only minutes earlier. There was time for only five or six exchanges on the radio-telephone between the pilot and controller in which to
55 give directions and speeds.

As the Jumbo sped down the runway, three tyres burst and others were deflated by the **excessive weight**. But ambulances
60 standing by were not needed and

the passengers were swiftly and safely evacuated from the aircraft. It was only after the

65 incident was over that Peter Bish was able to spare a thought for those passengers.

From *The Observer Magazine*, Young Observer section (abridged)

Exercise 1

In reading narrative, it is important to keep in mind the order of events.

Without looking at the passage, rearrange the following in the correct chronological order. Then check your order with the passage.

1 The engine caught fire.
2 Three tyres blew up on the aircraft.
3 Bish saw the aircraft on his radar screen.
4 Bish told his supervisor about the emergency.
5 The passengers were taken off the aircraft.
6 The supervisor informed the local fire brigades.
7 Bish was told of the emergency.
8 Bish guided the pilot towards the landing.
9 The pilot told the air traffic control centre about the fire.
10 The aircraft stopped safely.

Exercise 2

Choose the most likely meaning of these words in the context of the passage. Refer to the hints given in brackets if you are not sure of the answers.

1 **bound for** (line 9): *a* tied to *b* going towards (A place?)
2 **plight** (line 18): *a* a serious situation *b* horror (Calmly informed?)
3 **gusting** (line 27): *a* blowing *b* falling (*From the east?*)
4 **the cockpit** (line 31): *a* the pilot's area *b* the passengers' area
5 **histrionics** (line 33): *a* special machines *b* overexcited reactions (In the control tower?)
6 **the supervisor** (line 36): was ranked *a* above Bish *b* below Bish
7 **apron** (line 42): *a* something worn *b* a place of a similar shape (Runway?)
8 **deflated** (line 58): *a* blown up *b* let down

Exercise 3

Find words or phrases in the passage that are similar in meaning to the following. The number in brackets indicates the paragraph where the word or phrase is to be found.

1 stated (2)
2 informed (3)
3 rang (5)
4 speeding (5)
5 spotted (6)
6 raced (7)
7 waiting in readiness (7)

Escape from the fire

Arkady pulled the major up and lifted him onto a shoulder. He could no longer see the tractor or trees or sun. He started to his left, the last clear path he recalled.

Weaving under the weight of Pribluda, tripping on debris, soon 5 he couldn't tell if he was moving left, right or in a circle, but he knew that they would die if he stopped. It was the claustrophobia of not breathing, of keeping his mouth shut as if there were a hand over it, that he hadn't expected. When he could go no further and was so deep in smoke that he had to shut his eyes entirely, he ordered himself 10 another twenty steps, and when the smoke was worse, another twenty steps beyond that and then another ten, and another five. He stumbled into a ditch of brackish water. The ditch was as tall as a man; the water was shallow, and between it and the lip of the ditch lay a channel of thin, acrid air. Pribluda's lips were violet. Arkady 15 turned him on his back in the water and rocked back and forth, pumping air into him. Pribluda revived but the heat became worse.

The ditch rose and ended, and at first in the haze Arkady thought he had worked his way back to the field he had started from that morning. Then he saw that the **excavation machines**, water tanks 20 and fire engines were black and gutted, some upended from explosions when their fuel ignited, and that what seemed shapeless hillocks on a charred field were the bodies of men who had died the day before. From two of the bodies Arkady took intact water containers, made masks out of his shirt, wet them, tied them on 25 Pribluda and himself, and started out again as the smoke approached.

Finally they came to a **palisade** of burned trees. 'There's no place left to go, the smoke is everywhere.' Pribluda watched the encircling darkness. 'Why did you lead us here? See, the trees are burning 30 again.'

'That's not smoke, it's night. Those are stars,' Arkady said. 'We're safe.'

excavation machines: used for digging

palisade: The line of burned trees were like the upright parts of a fence.

From *Gorky Park* by Martin Cruz Smith (abridged)

Exercise 1

It is sometimes difficult on first reading an extract from a book to understand what is going on.

Find evidence in the text to support the following suppositions.
1 The major was injured.
2 Arkady was lost, because of the smoke.
3 He did not see the ditch.
4 The major could hardly breathe.
5 Many men had died trying to put out the fire.
6 Some of the fire engines had turned over when the fuel blew up.
7 They reached safety because the fire had already passed over that place. ·

Exercise 2

Choose the most likely meaning of these words in the context of the passage.
1 **weaving** (line 4): *a* making cloth *b* moving from side to side?
2 **debris** (line 4): *a* plants *b* wreckage after a disaster
3 **brackish** (line 13): tastes *a* bitter *b* sweet?
4 **acrid** (line 15): *a* pure *b* unpleasant to the nose and mouth?
5 **hillocks** (line 23): *a* heaps *b* slopes?
6 **masks** (line 25): protected *a* their chests *b* their faces

Exercise 3

Find words or phrases in the passage that are similar in meaning to the following. The number in brackets indicates the paragraph where the word or phrase is to be found.
1 stumbling (2)
2 closed (2)
3 completely (2)
4 edge (2)
5 recovered (2)
6 burnt out (3) (2 words)
7 caught fire (3)
8 undamaged (3)
9 at last (4)

Exercise 4

● **A   arise (arose, arisen), raise (raised, raised), rise (rose, risen)**

Only **raise** can have an object. **Arise** is used to mean 'come into being'.
e.g.   New problems are arising every day.

*Use the correct form of **raise** or **rise** in the following sentences.*
1 The Government has just _____ taxes, and prices are _____, too.
2 Arkady _____ the major to his feet.
3 They _____ when she came in.
4 His temperature has _____ since last night.
5 All my family were _____ on porridge for breakfast and I'll _____ my children the same way.

● **B   lay (laid, laid), lie (lay, lain)**

Lay has an object; **lie** does not.

*Use the correct form of **lay** or **lie** in the following sentences.*
1 He _____ in a ditch and I _____ his coat on top of him.
2 The smoke _____ between Arkady and safety.
3 _____ down, and you'll feel better!
4 _____ it on the table, please!
5 The choice _____ in whether there is an object or not.

● **C   fog, haze, mist, smoke, steam**

Choose the correct word to complete the following.
1 _____ is like a cloud near the surface of the earth; _____ is the same, but less thick.
2 Boiling water produces _____, but fires produce _____.
3 Hot weather sometimes creates a_____, which makes it difficult for us to see clearly.
4 Smog is a form of industrial pollution, a mixture of _____ and _____. (It is a word formed by two others in the list.)

Unusual people

Introductory exercise

Before looking at the passage below, say whether these general statements are true or false.

1 If you have a cockney accent, you probably come from London.
2 Apart from English, three other languages are spoken by natives of the British Isles.
3 An idiom means the same thing as a language.
4 The English spoken on the BBC is a dialect.
5 The most important speech at a wedding reception in Britain is made by the bridegroom.

The modern Professor Higgins

'You can spot an Irishman or a Yorkshireman by his brogue,' says Professor Higgins in *Pygmalion*. 'I can place any man
5 within six miles. I can place him within two miles in London. Sometimes within two streets.' Sceptics may have thought Shaw was imagining such a character, that
10 the trick was impossible: but in fact he based Higgins on several distinguished 'phoneticians' of the time, and the trick can allegedly still be done.
15 Stanley Ellis of the University of Leeds is a modern Higgins. The police have often asked for Mr Ellis's help, usually as an expert witness identifying the voice in a
20 bomb hoax or fire calls.
Former Detective Inspector Mick Turner, who was in charge of the Scientific Aids Section at Nottingham and has worked on
25 cases with him, says, 'I was very impressed with Stanley. His knowledge is fantastic. He taught us a lot and gave us good advice on how to prepare a case against someone
30 using this evidence. But it worked both ways. On another occasion when we had a suspect he said straightaway, "Don't waste your time. That's not him!" And of
35 course the evidence later proved that he was right. So he saved us a lot of time.'
Ellis says his evidence is always corroborative, never conclusive.
40 The real experts, he says, are not academics but the local people; they can detect infallibly the **nuances**, **topographical** and social, of the speech patterns around their homes.
45 The English Department at Leeds has been working for more than 30 years on a huge dialect survey accumulating great masses of material from all over England.
50 Because of its reputation in this field Leeds was the ultimate beneficiary of George Bernard Shaw's eccentric bequest for the invention of a new phonetic alphabet.
55 A special typewriter was actually built and was on display there, but the alphabet has never been used.
The **Shavian** alphabet may lack supporters, but general interest in
60 accents and dialects has increased enormously, Ellis says. Whenever strangers find out what Ellis does, the conversation immediately starts to flow. It is a subject on which
65 almost everybody has opinions, often vehement ones.

nuances: subtle differences
topographical: regional

Shavian: relating to George Bernard Shaw

From *Ellis, The Modern Higgins* by Anthony Lejeune in the *Sunday Telegraph Magazine* (abridged)

Exercise 1

Multiple-choice questions for reading comprehension usually consist of four statements: three of them are false, and recognising that they are false depends on careful reading. It is necessary to say to yourself: 'No, the passage doesn't say that, exactly. It says something else'. As in the following example, this is often a matter of logic.

Compare these statements.
e.g. Higgins claims he can place:
    a any man's accent within two miles.
    b any Londoner's accent within two streets.
    c any Londoner's accent within six miles.
    All of these statements are false, because he does not *claim* any of them, but only what is stated in the text. But if the introduction read 'Higgins can place ...', one would be correct. Why?

Prove the following statements about the passage false.
1 The police always ask Mr Ellis's help as an expert witness.
2 Mr Ellis's knowledge is always used to prepare cases against suspects.
3 Local people know more about phonetics than Mr Ellis.
4 Mr Ellis often works on cases with Detective Inspector Turner.
5 Leeds University did not make any use of Shaw's bequest.

Exercise 2

● A

Find words or phrases in the passage that are similar in meaning to the following. The number in brackets indicates the paragraph where the word or phrase is to be found.
1 recognise (1)
2 dialect (1)
3 false alarm (2)
4 responsible for (3)
5 used to confirm (4)
6 collecting (5)
7 discover (7)
8 strong (7)

● B

Find terms in the passage for people who:
1 doubt the truth of something
2 study pronunciation
3 provide evidence
4 are thought to have committed a crime
5 know a great deal about a subject
6 receive something when someone dies

Exercise 3

● A   **guide, instruct, learn, teach, train**

*Use each verb, **at least once**, in the correct form to complete the following.*
1 Mr Ellis _____ the police a lot. They _____ from him how to prepare cases, using the evidence of voices and accents.
2 Mr Ellis _____ phonetics at Leeds University. He _____ students on the frequency of certain speech patterns and they are _____ (2 possibilities) to recognise them.
3 There are schools where blind people are _____ how to use guide dogs. The dogs are _____ (2 possibilities) to _____ them through traffic.

● B   **chance, luck, occasion, opportunity, possibility**

Study these sentences.
e.g. Good **luck**! I hope you win.
    Is there any **chance/possibility** of solving the crime?
    The **opportunity/chance** of winning a million pounds was too good to miss, so he **took a chance/risk** and won. What **luck**!
    On another **occasion**, quite **by chance** (=without looking for it), he found a gold watch in the street.
    I hope to have **the opportunity of visiting** Canada soon.
    I may have **occasion** (=reason) **to visit** Canada soon.

Choose the correct word to complete the following.

On one ¹_____, Mr Ellis was asked to help the police identify a murderer who made phone calls. There was a ²_____ (2 possibilities) that his knowledge would be useful. The police had several ³_____ (2 possibilities) to test his theory about the murderer, but in fact he was caught by ⁴_____, when a young policeman saw a van suspiciously parked. On this ⁵_____, the arrest was more a matter of ⁶_____ than judgement.

The funeral of Harry Lime

It was just chance that they found the funeral in time – one patch in the enormous park where the snow had been shovelled aside and a tiny group was gathered, apparently bent on some very private business. A priest had finished speaking, his words coming
5 secretively through the thin patient snow, and a coffin was on the point of being lowered into the ground. Two men in lounge suits stood at the graveside; one carried a wreath that he obviously had forgotten to drop on to the coffin, for his companion nudged his elbow so that he came to with a start and dropped the flowers. A girl
10 stood a little way away with her hands over her face, and I stood twenty yards away by another grave, watching with relief the last of Lime and noticing carefully who was there – just a man in a mackintosh I was to Martins. He came up to me and said, 'Could you tell me who they are burying?'
15 'A fellow called Lime,' I said, and was astonished to see the tears start to this stranger's eyes: he didn't look like a man who wept, nor was Lime the kind of man whom I thought likely to have mourners – genuine mourners with genuine tears. There was the girl of course, but one excepts women from all such
20 generalisations.

came to: here, became aware of his surroundings again after being lost in thought; also regained consciousness

From *The Third Man* by Graham Greene

Exercise 1

● A

Real comprehension of a passage depends on understanding it in depth.

Answer these questions on the passage. Find phrases to support your answers.

1   What were the attitudes towards Lime's death of: **a** Martins; **b** the girl; **c** the two men in lounge suits; **d** the narrator? How do you know?
2   The narrator is a policeman in plain clothes. Which phrases suggest this?
3   Which of the characters had only just found out about the funeral? Which two phrases tell us this?
4   What relationship do you imagine existed between Lime and: **a** the girl; **b** Martins; **c** the narrator? Why do you think so?

● B

At the same time, it is dangerous to use your imagination too much and assume things that are not necessarily true.

Say if the following statements are true or false, only on the basis of what the passage indicates.

1   The funeral was private, and Martins had been excluded from it.
2   The two men in lounge suits did not like Lime.
3   The girl was not really upset by Lime's death.
4   The narrator had never met Martins before.
5   The narrator thought Lime might have had a lover, but no friends.
6   Harry Lime was dead.

Exercise 2

Use words from the passage to complete this description of a funeral.

At a ¹_____, the body is carried in a ²_____ and lowered into the ³_____. The ⁴_____ accompanying the body usually bring a ⁵_____ of flowers. After ⁶_____ the body, earth is ⁷_____ over it.

Exercise 3

Find words or phrases in the passage that are similar in meaning to the following. The number in brackets indicates the paragraph where the word or phrase is to be found.

1   a small area (1)
2   concentrating (1)
3   touched gently (1)
4   became awake (1)
5   surprised (2)

Exercise 4

● **particular, peculiar, personal, private**

Replace the words or phrases in italic with one of these adjectives. Put them in front of the appropriate noun.

1   Have you any *special* reason for asking that question?
2   He has employed a teacher *just for himself.*
3   She looked at me in a *strange* way.
4   He asked for an interview with the boss *in person.*
5   This is a party *not open to people in general.*
6   Transport in this town belongs to companies *that do not belong to the state or the local council.*

Lexical Progress Test 1

You must choose the word or phrase which best completes each sentence. For each question, 1 to 25, indicate the correct answer, A, B, C or D. The time for the test is 20 minutes. NOTE: A few words of advice. Do not try to answer the questions by translating into your own language. This will almost certainly produce a wrong answer. If you are in doubt, read the sentence to yourself, including each possibility in turn, until you think you recognise the form of the phrase. Do not hurry. You have more time than you imagine. But do not spend a long time over one question. Go on to the next, and then come back to any that you have not answered at the end.

1 _____ the flight times before you book the tickets.
A Check B Control C Inform D Prove

2 I _____ you to be at the party this evening.
A expect B hope C look forward to D wait

3 I arranged to meet a Mr Jones here. I hope I haven't _____ him.
A avoided B lacked C lost D missed

4 We were at school together, but it took me a long time to _____ her.
A find B get to know C know D meet

5 Where do you _____ the writing paper? In this drawer?
A close B guard C hold D keep

6 British Airways _____ the departure of Flight 123 to Palma.
A advertises B advises C announces D notices

7 He lives in this building, on the third _____.
A flat B floor C level D stage

8 He was badly _____ in a car accident.
A damaged B harmed C hurt D wounded

9 My shoes are worn out. I'll have to buy a new _____.
A couple B ones C pair D set

10 He was sitting on the river _____, fishing.
A bank B border C cliff D shore

11 If you need any help this evening, _____ us.
A count on B put up C stand with D trust for

12 When he's 65, he'll _____ with a good pension.
A resign B retire C sack D withdraw

13 He _____ guests to dinner almost every night.
A amuses B claims C entertains D greets

14 It takes time to get used to living in a hot _____.
A air B climate C season D weather

15 The school _____ begins on October 1st.
A period B season C term D time

16 Their prompt action prevented the fire from _____.
A flowing B scattering C spilling D spreading

17 The hotel _____ us five pounds for the room.
A afforded B charged C cost D demanded

18 How much is the _____ to Madrid, travelling first class?
A bill B expense C fare D fee

19 He _____ to listen to my arguments, and walked away.
A denied B disliked C objected D refused

20 This girl was to _____ the most important person in his life.
A become B develop C grow up D result

21 There's no one at home _____, but I expect Mother will be back soon.
A actually B at present C currently D presently

22 New problems are _____ every day in this company.
A arising B going up C raising D rising

23 He was _____ on the ground, quite still.
A lain B lied C laying D lying

24 She couldn't see herself in the mirror because of the _____ rising from the hot bath.
A fog B mist C smoke D steam

25 I don't think we have much _____ of winning today.
A chance B luck C occasion D opportunity

City and country

Introductory exercise

Before looking at the passage below, answer these questions.

1 Houses built in rows are called **terraced**. What are they called if built: **a** in rows of two houses together; **b** standing alone?

2 Would you find the following inside or outside a building: **a** a balcony; **b** a lift; **c** stairs; **d** steps; **e** a yard?

3 What would you keep in: **a** a cellar; **b** a garage; **c** a larder; **d** a shed; **e** a stable?

A spa in the heart of London

Sadler's Wells, originally a holy well, was rediscovered and developed as a **spa** and pleasure garden by Mr Sadler in the eighteenth century. In time, a theatre was added – the springs are still in existence under it.

My favourite approach is northwards from St James's Walk behind Clerkenwell Church through streets of well-proportioned terraces. Fine doors and balconies occur here and there, but the quarter has a somewhat crestfallen air, as if it knew it belonged properly to Bloomsbury, but had got itself dislocated and unfashionable through an error of judgement. Halfway to Sadler's Wells, one crosses the end of Exmouth Market with the pub, 'The London Spa', marking the site of yet another and minor spa, at the corner.

Alongside the theatre is Arlington Way, a charming street of small **Georgian** terraced houses with shops below. There is also a curious old stable yard with grass-grown **cobbles** and hollyhocks, a relic of the days of donkey and pony carts, and a **choice** half-pint size pub, 'The Harlequin'.

Where Arlington Way joins Chadwell Street is a new four-storey block with its main **elevation** on St John Street; it is in the Georgian style and of remarkable quality and is an example of what can be done when a civilised scheme to harmonise with existing work takes precedence over an ambition to create something new and exciting.

spa: a resort where people go to take the mineral waters
Georgian: from the time of George IV (1820–30)

cobbles: small, rounded paving stones
choice: here, exceptionally good
elevation: here, height, visible features

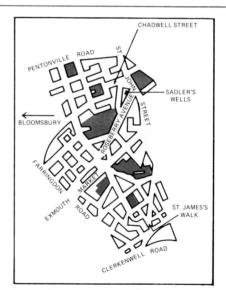

From *Capital Spas* by Geoffrey Fletcher in the *Daily Telegraph* (abridged)

Exercise 1

Use the passage and the map to answer the following questions.

1 Trace the writer's probable route from St. James's Walk to Sadler's Wells.

2 Mark: **a** 'The London Spa'; **b** Arlington Way; **c** the new four-storey block.

3 How many parks or open spaces would the writer pass? On his left or his right?

Exercise 2

Choose the most likely meaning of these words or phrases in the context of the passage.

1 **crestfallen** (line 15): *a* depressed *b* with damaged roofs
2 **dislocated** (line 18): *a* replaced *b* out of its true position
3 **hollyhocks** (line 32): are *a* a kind of stone *b* flowers
4 **a half-pint size pub** (line 34): *a* a pub which serves half-pints *b* a very small pub
5 **takes precedence over** (line 45): *a* is considered socially superior *b* receives prior consideration

Exercise 3

Find words or phrases in the passage that are similar in meaning to the following. The number in brackets indicates the paragraph where the word or phrase is to be found.

1 at one time (1)
2 later (1)
3 rather (2)
4 mistake (in) (2)
5 indicating (2)
6 less important (2)
7 strange (3)
8 survivor (3)
9 principal (4)
10 plan (4)

Introductory exercise

Before looking at the passage below, check that you know the following terms.
Do you know the difference between: *a* a primary school; *b* a secondary school; *c* a grammar school; *d* a comprehensive school; *e* a boarding school?

A country childhood

My beginnings were like those of a country child in the eighteenth century. The self-containment of the village, its environment, its self-dependence — the whole situation, all were different. And I was different there. We had a little farm which went down, down, down.
5   Our poverty was dreadful and extreme, and nobody believed that it would ever go away. Now and then it rose up and struck at me personally and there was absolutely nothing that I could do about it. Or Mother, and she had learnt ways of dealing with practically everything.
10   It was Mother who found the way out. Had she not discovered it, my entire life would have been different. I would have left school at twelve or so and become a farm-labourer. Mother heard that an old charity existed in the village which allowed the sum of £10 to educate one boy for one year. One year's education, of course, was no good to
15 anyone. But this charity had been ignored and neglected for so long that a substantial balance had built up. And so first my brother and then myself got to the grammar school and stayed there, backed by this ancient money. Mother's determination — she would have moved heaven and earth to make the trustees start paying this charity
20 again — altered everything. It made all the difference in the world to my life. It completely re-routed it. Certainly without it I should have been at work on the land and with all the lack of chances which went with such an existence at that time.

The grammar school itself was still stuck in some distant past. It consisted mainly of a seventeenth-century hall with a curtain down the middle to make two classrooms — a very hit-and-miss sort of division with the noise and tensions, and the scrape of two different classes grinding against each other. Half a mile away there was the headmaster's house and another classroom and a gymnasium. There were about twenty boys and two or three teachers. Some of us were boarders and quite a lot of people walked in daily from all the surrounding country villages. One boy rode in on a pony and stabled it at the pub opposite the school. The whole situation was still essentially Tudor. It was surprising what we all managed in such primitive conditions, with no science lab, no specialist teachers bar the headmaster, and a games field which was just a rough meadow. There was only one prize day all the time I was there and that was thought quite an innovation.

From *The View in Winter* by Ronald Blythe (abridged)

Exercise 1

Choose the most likely meaning of these words in the context of the passage.

1 **self-containment** (line 2): *a* control of emotion *b* completeness in itself
2 **charity** (line 13): is *a* a kindness *b* money provided to help people
3 **ignored** (line 15): suggests *a* no one knew about the charity *b* no one paid any attention to it
4 **the trustees** (line 19): were responsible for administering *a* the charity *b* the school
5 **hit-and-miss** (line 26): *a* inconsistent and unpredictable *b* occasionally violent

3 Without the charity, the writer would have had to
  a work on a farm.
  b stay in the village.
  c leave school early.
4 The grammar school had
  a one classroom.
  b two classrooms.
  c three classrooms.
  (How many of these answers can possibly be correct?)
5 Some children
  a lived at the school in term time.
  b left their ponies there.
  c walked long distances to school.

Exercise 2

*Compare each of the statements below with the passage and decide whether they are true or false. In each group, **one** or **two** may be correct.*

1 The writer's childhood was like that of a boy in the eighteenth century because
  a his father owned a farm.
  b the village formed its own world.
  c the farm was not profitable.
2 His life changed because
  a the trustees offered to pay for his education.
  b there was enough money to educate one boy for a year.
  c the village charity had accumulated a lot of money.

Exercise 3

Find words or phrases in the passage that are similar in meaning to the following. The number in brackets indicates the paragraph where the word or phrase is to be found.

1 terrible (2)
2 almost (2)
3 changed (3)
4 whole (3)
5 considerable (3)
6 supported (3)
7 old (3)
8 fixed (4)
9 except (4)
10 field (4)

Exercise 4

● A forget, leave, neglect, omit

*Use each verb, **at least once**, in the correct form to complete the following.*

1   *a* Oh dear! I've _____ my books.
    b Oh dear! I've _____ my books at home.
2   How old were you when you _____ school?
3   I've _____ all the Latin I learned at school.
4   If you _____ your work, you can't hope to pass the exam.
5   You haven't filled in the form completely. You've _____ your name.

● B allow, leave, let

Use these verbs in the correct form to complete the following.

1   *a* They don't _____ you smoke here.
    b You aren't _____ to smoke here.
    c We don't _____ smoking here.
    d We don't _____ people to smoke here.
2   *a* I'll _____ you stay up late tonight.
    b I'll _____ you to stay up late tonight.
3   Don't worry about the washing-up! _____ it to me.
4   Children shouldn't be _____ alone in the house at the age of three.

● C crusty, raw, rough, rude, rusty, tough

Use one of these adjectives to describe each of the following.

1   **behaviour** that is impolite
2   **bread** with a firm outer covering
3   a **chain** left out in the rain
4   an **idea** that is not yet exact
5   **materials** before processing
6   **meat** that hasn't been cooked
7   **meat** that is hard to eat
8   **play** that is strong and determined
9   **play** that is unfair
10 **shoes** that are hard-wearing
11 a **surface** that is uneven
12 unpleasant **weather**

Finding the way

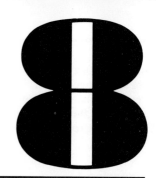

Introductory exercise

Before looking at the passage below, answer these questions.

1 What do you understand by: ***a*** one-way street; ***b*** a main road; ***c*** a side road; ***d*** the roadside; ***e*** a through road; ***f*** a square; ***g*** a roundabout; ***h*** a motorway?

2 Distinguish between: ***a*** a city; ***b*** a town; ***c*** a village; ***d*** a suburb; ***e*** the outskirts.

A small town 40 years ago

We lived on the outskirts of the town where I grew up, with open fields at the top of the hill, but the town centre was quite near, too, because most of the building had taken place in the opposite direction; I suppose this was because the county boundary was only a mile away, to the south.

Our house was on the bend of a short crescent-shaped road which curved round to join two parallel roads out of town, one that led to a few nearby villages and the other to London. On their way into town, they still ran parallel, but changed their names, the former to Chapel Street, after the Methodist chapel, the latter to Castle Street, though there was no castle left to remind us of its original owner, Fulk the Brute.

Chapel Street led into the main street, George Street, which ran for about 100 yards at right angles to it turning left. At our end of George Street, on a triangular island, was the Corn Exchange; at one time farmers used it to sell the harvest. On our side of the triangle was Market Hill, joining Chapel Street and Castle Street. At the far end of George Street, facing the Corn Exchange, was the Town Hall, an imposing modern building, with the War Memorial (for the 1914–18 War) in front of it, and on either side of it two streets forming a fork that soon became the main roads to Dunstable, on the left, and Bedford, on the right.

George Street was not named after the reigning king, George VI, but after George IV, who had happened to be on the throne when it was built. The contemporary national hero, the Duke of Wellington, was also commemorated by a street at right angles to George Street, next to the Town Hall and parallel to Chapel Street. Later monarchs had not fared so well, though the town had obviously done the best it could, naming the first available street after them as building progressed. Victoria Street was a little

street halfway up Castle Street and Chapel Street, and where
these changed their names to London Road and Farley Hill
respectively, someone had had the bright idea of taking in the
whole of the present family at one go by naming the next
35 connecting road Windsor Street.

Exercise 1

*Use the information given in this passage to
draw a map, showing all the streets and
buildings mentioned. Remember that George
Street is in the north, and the hill leading out of
town to London is in the south-east.*

Exercise 2

*Find words or phrases in the passage that are
similar in meaning to the following. The
number in brackets indicates the paragraph
where the word or phrase is to be found.*
1   neighbouring (2)
2   the first-mentioned (2)
3   the last-mentioned (2)
4   reigning (4)
5   kings and queens (4)
6   been so fortunate (4)
7   in that order (4)
8   all at once (4)

Exercise 3

● **A   border, boundary, division, edge, limit,
line**

Many words are very similar in meaning, but
we associate a particular one with certain
contexts.

*Which of these words do you associate with the
contexts referred to below?*
1   a **cliff**
2   **clothes** hanging up
3   a division between **countries**
4   a division between two pieces of **land**
5   **flowers** around grass
6   part of a **company**
7   a **handkerchief**
8   a **knife**
9   a **loan** from the bank
10 **mathematics**
11 **patience**
12 the **route** of a railway
13 **telephones**
14 where **trains** run
15 **poetry**

● **B   commemorate, memorise, remember,
remind**

*Use each verb, **at least once**, in the correct
form to complete the following.*
1   Do you _____ that party at Sarah's last
year?
— Yes, now that you _____ me. I _____
driving home in the snow.
It _____ me of Christmas in my childhood.
2   Wellington Street _____ the Duke of
Wellington.
3   I'm _____ my lines for the school play. I
hope I _____ them on the night.
4   _____ to post that letter tomorrow. It's very
important.
— OK. But _____ me to post it in the
morning. I may forget.

A house called 'The Franchise'

Two miles out on the Larborough road stood the house known as The Franchise, set down by the roadside with the **inconsequence** of a telephone kiosk. In the last days of **the Regency** someone had bought the field known as The Franchise, built in the middle of it a flat white
5 house, and then surrounded the whole with a high, solid wall of brick with a large double gate, of wall height, in the middle of the road frontage. It had no relation with anything in the countryside: no farm buildings in the background; no side-gates, even, into the surrounding fields. Stables were built, in accordance with the period, at the back
0 of the house, but they were inside the wall. The place was as irrelevant, as isolated as a child's toy dropped by the wayside. It had been occupied as long as Robert could remember by an old man, presumably the same old man; but since The Franchise people had always shopped at Ham Green, the village on the Larborough side of
5 them, they had never been seen in Milford. And then Marion Sharpe and her mother had begun to be part of the morning shopping scene in Milford, and it was understood that they had inherited The Franchise when the old man died.

inconsequence: The writer suggests there is no logical reason for the choice of site for telephone kiosks.
the Regency: 1810–20, when the Prince Regent, later George IV, ruled in place of his father, George III.

From *The Franchise Affair* by Josephine Tey

Exercise 1

Warning: This map is not accurate. Do not use it to interpret the text of the passage.

Most of the details in this map are wrong. When you have read the text, point out the mistakes that have been made.

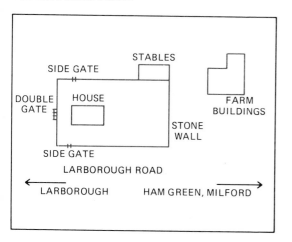

Exercise 2

*Of the following statements, only **one** is correct in each case. Compare each of them with the text, and decide why the others are false.*

1 The Franchise
   a had been built near a telephone kiosk.
   b was on the outskirts of Larborough.
   c did not fit in with its surroundings.
2 The people who had lived at The Franchise before the Sharpes
   a always shopped at a village on the way to Milford.
   b did not come to Milford because they shopped in the opposite direction.
   c were often seen shopping in Milford in the mornings.
3 The last sentence in the passage means that
   a the old man had told the shopkeepers in Milford about his will.
   b people got the idea that the Sharpes had been left the house in his will.
   c Robert knew about the relationship between the Sharpes and the old man.

Discussion

Introductory exercise

Before looking at the passage below, answer these questions.

1 When driving a car, when would you use:
   a the accelerator; **b** the brake; **c** the clutch;
   d the steering wheel; **e** the boot?

2 Where would you find: **a** a crossroads;
   b a level crossing; **c** traffic lights?

3 What is the purpose of: **a** traffic signs;
   b signposts; **c** L-plates; **d** a parking meter;
   e a zebra crossing; **f** a ring road; **g** a speed
   limit?

Seat belts: freedom and the law

TOMORROW it becomes a criminal offence to drive a car in Great Britain while not wearing a seat belt.

5 Although this is a political question it is not a party-political one. Some Tories have consistently voted for seat belts, some Labour **Members** against; it is not a Socialist enthusiasm, nor Tory-authoritarian. It is the authentic voice of the **Nanny** State, kind, well-intentioned, looking after us and telling us what we may or may not do, all for our own good.

Its beauty as a political topic is its simplicity. Here in the purest form is the question: should the State interfere with and limit an individual's freedom of action even when the deleterious consequences of such action affect no one else?

25 Anti-belters have sometimes fudged the issue and put forward empirical or practical arguments against the compulsory wearing of seat belts. That is all beside the point. Better to admit that wearing a seat belt is good and sensible, not wearing one bad and foolish (for what it's worth I wear one myself). But should we be *made* to do the sensible thing? Is not a fatal principle conceded?

Some belters-up would say that it is by no means a simple case of the individual doing harm to himself which concerns no one else: a solitary motorist who drives into a lamppost and smashes himself up becomes a burden on society when he is taken to hospital; society, acting through the State, is entitled to guard against this burden.

But the argument is fraught with danger. Certainly there are victims of beltless car crashes in hospital wards. For that matter the casual connection between cigarette smoking and disease is well established. Is that a reason for banning cigarettes?

'The Nanny State' is a good phrase (**Iain Macleod's**, I think). Nannies are excellent people – for children. The mark of a truly free society is that, even if we don't always behave like grown-ups, the State treats us as if we were. Otherwise we are being, precisely, infantilised.

Members: Members of Parliament, MPs

nanny: child's nurse employed in rich households

Iain Macleod: a Conservative minister who died in 1970

From *When nanny says 'Belt Up'* by Geoffrey Wheatcroft in the *Sunday Telegraph* (abridged)

34

Exercise 1

Choose the most likely meaning of these words or phrases in the context of the passage.
1 **empirical** (line 27): *a* theoretical *b* based on experience
2 **for what it's worth** (line 33): *a* as a matter of fact *b* because of its great value (Which is more likely for this writer, considering his views?)
3 **a solitary motorist** (line 41): is *a* lonely *b* alone in the car
4 **smashes himself up** (line 43): *a* kills himself *b* is badly injured (Hospital?)
5 **infantilised** (line 64): *a* made fun of *b* transformed into children

Exercise 2

Understanding an argument is a matter of recognising the points made in favour and against, and seeing which of these are the writer's.

Decide which of the following are the writer's own opinions.
He thinks that:
1 the State's intentions are good.
2 the State should tell people what to do for their own good.
3 the practical arguments against seat belts are valid.
4 it is sensible to wear a seat belt.
5 he himself would never wear one.
6 seat belts should not be made compulsory.
7 society has a right to protect itself against careless drivers.
8 there is a connection between cigarette smoking and disease.
9 cigarette smoking should be forbidden.
10 the State should assume people are responsible, whether they are or not.

Exercise 3

It is also important to recognise which are the main points of a writer's argument, and which are details.

Group the following in two groups, main arguments and secondary arguments.
1 The political parties do not agree among themselves about seat belts.
2 The State should not interfere with individual freedom unless it harms other people.
3 There are practical arguments against wearing seat belts.
4 The State must accept the responsibility for people injured in car crashes, whether they were wearing seat belts or not.
5 A free society must treat its citizens as responsible people.

Exercise 4

Find words or phrases in the passage that are similar in meaning to the following. The number in brackets indicates the paragraph where the word or phrase is to be found.
1 real (2)
2 harmful (3)
3 confused (4)
4 obligatory (4)
5 irrelevant (4)
6 granted (4)
7 heavy responsibility (5)
8 full (of) (6)
9 forbidding (6)
10 adults (7)

Exercise 5

● A **sensational, senseless, sensible, sensitive**

Choose the correct word to complete the following.
Every Christmas the popular press publishes
¹_____ figures about road accidents. These
touch a ²_____ nerve in most drivers, who can
no longer enjoy themselves at parties. Of course
it is ³_____ not to drink too much, but most
accidents are caused by the ⁴_____ madmen
who drive the same way all the time. Still, the
campaign may have made motorists more
⁵_____ to criticism and reduced accidents
because many take the ⁶_____ course and stay
overnight with friends instead of driving home.

● **B   fatal, grave, serious, slight, solemn**

Which of these words cannot be used to describe an accident or illness?
Place those words describing an accident or illness in order of seriousness.

Readers' letters: seat belts

LETTERS TO THE EDITOR

Naughty to defy nanny?

1 In his article on the compulsory wearing of seat belts, Geoffrey Wheatcroft asks 'Should we be made to do the sensible thing? Is not a fatal principle conceded?'

In fact, this principle – the freedom of the individual – was conceded ten years ago, when, in June 1973, Mr Heath's Government introduced the compulsory wearing of crash helmets for motorcyclists. It was only a matter of time before motorists suffered a similar infringement of their liberty.
DAVID J. PEARSON,
Pensly, Merseyside.

2 Mr Wheatcroft's argument leads logically to the banning of any regulations related to personal safety, for example in the field of industry. Do the anti-belters really want that?

The passenger who refuses to obey the airline stewardess at take-off and landing is a rarity simply because, once it is emphasised, the reasonableness of the regulations is apparent to all. I suspect that the same applies to motorists and will be shown to do so.
(Professor)   J.K.   MASON (Scottish   Sub-Committee Medical   Commission   on Accident   Prevention), Edinburgh.

3 As regards the cost to the tax-payer of treating the victims of road accidents, may I suggest a form of compulsory insurance, which would be waived for people prepared to sign an undertaking always to wear a seat belt, in much the same way that one life insurance company offers reduced premiums to non-smokers?
W.M. AGG, Acklam, Yorks.
From the *Sunday Telegraph* (abridged)

'WH
WIT

Every year, W
for housebuildin
But this year,
recipients.

From the *Sunday Telegraph* (abridged)

Exercise 1

Answer these questions on the letters to the newspaper.

1   Decide in each case whether the letter: **a** supports the point of view in the original article; **b** disagrees with it; **c** offers a third suggestion. In the last case, would this suggestion contradict the basic argument of the article? Give reasons for your choice.
2   In what way does the first letter add information to the article?
3   What is the justification in the article for the first sentence of the second letter?
4   What is the point of the comparison between seat belts and flying, and why is it appropriate? (Think of the stewardess's instruction.)
5   Do you think the suggestion in the third letter would be effective?

Exercise 2

*Explain why the word **naughty** is used in the headline, instead of **bad, evil** or **wicked**. Place the four adjectives in order of seriousness.*

Exercise 3

Find words or phrases in the letters that are similar in meaning to the following. The number in brackets indicates the letter where the word or phrase is to be found.

1   an illegal restriction (on) (1)
2   with reference to (3)
3   not insisted on (3)
4   a legally enforceable promise (3)
5   money paid to an insurance company (3)

Readers' letters: the police and the public

1 WITH reference to Jonathan Sumption's article 'Why the police are losing public support', it appears that he thinks that more police time is used on trivial offences, motoring offences and the like.

It may not matter to you if your neighbour has not displayed a car tax disc, but probably the reason he has no disc is because he has no insurance certificate either. If, therefore, he were to hit your wife driving down the road and your car was **a write-off**, you would have no chance of claiming on his insurance even if it was his fault.

CHRISTINA KELLOW,
Devizes, Wilts.

a write-off: a total wreck, beyond repair

2 I THINK Jonathan Sumption makes a wrong assumption in one respect. He says that **'prefects** cannot possibly be deferential', inferring that the police when dealing with the public, especially over so-called 'minor' offences to do with motoring, cannot be respectful.

I contend that they can and they don't, by and large, and have therefore forfeited the *respect* of the public, which is essential to public support.

PATRICK TAILYOUR,
Great Easton, Lincs.

prefects: The article compared the police to senior school boys put in the charge of others

3 CONTRARY to Mr Sumption's views I do think ill of those who (continually) try to evade paying their fair share by whatever kind of tax dodging; I do think ill of those whose thoughtless parking causes at least inconvenience to others and frequently damage or personal injury from accidents involving other motorists trying to avoid a badly parked car.

Nor do I think it trivial to smoke marijuana or leave one's children unattended. Mr Sumption suggests many honest Englishmen support his views; I'd suggest many more do not. We are not prepared to let our standards slip – we'd prefer to raise them.

A.J. KERR,
Sendmarsh, Surrey.

From the *Sunday Telegraph*

Exercise 1

Study the letters and answer the following questions.

1 What was the subject of the original article?
2 What was the writer's argument? (Make a list of all the things the writer said which are mentioned here.)

3 Do the readers agree with the writer in general terms about the reasons for the police losing support?
4 Do they agree with him about other statements he made?
5 Do the letter-writers blame the police or the public for the present situation?

Exercise 2

● A

Find words or phrases in the letters that are similar in meaning to the following. The number in brackets indicates the letter where the word or phrase is to be found.

1   minor (1)
2   such things (1)
3   shown (1)
4   respectful (2)
5   argue (2)
6   in general (2)
7   lost (2)
8   get out of (3)
9   evasion (3)
10 fall (3)

● B

Answer these questions about the letters.

1   Why do you think 'minor' is printed in inverted commas in the second letter?
2   Which other phrase emphasises this point in the same sentence?

Exercise 3

● A   blame (*n. and v.*), defect, fail (*n. and v.*), fault

*Use each word, at least once, in the correct form to complete the following. **Blame** and **fail** are used both as nouns and as verbs.*

I thought there was something wrong with the brakes in my new car and complained to the garage about the ¹_____. Obviously, if the brakes ²_____, I would be in serious trouble. The garage people weren't prepared to take the ³_____. 'It's not our ⁴_____,' they said. 'The factory's to ⁵_____.' However, they promised to fix the brakes by Monday without ⁶_____. All the same, I do ⁷_____ the garage for not checking the car thoroughly before selling it.

● B   ask for, claim, demand, insist (on) require

Study these examples.

e.g.   I **asked** (him/the manager) **for** some money/help.
He **claimed** that his account of the accident was true.
He **claimed** the money (on his policy/from the insurance company).
I **demand** justice./I **demand** that you give me justice.
I **insist on** (knowing) the truth./I **insist** that you tell me the truth.
I **require** you/your presence at the meeting.

*Change the sentences below from Direct to Reported Speech. Use each of the verbs above, **at least once**, in the Past tense to introduce the sentence.*

1   'Please can you help me,' she said.
She _____ my ...
2   'We shall need you in court to give evidence.'
They said they would _____
3   'Tell me what's going on! I don't care how many times I have to ask you.'
She _____ ...what ...
4   'Give me the money, or I'll shoot you!'
I _____ the ...
5   'It's my money!'
She _____ the ...
6   'I'm telling the truth!'
He _____ that ...

Students' problems

Introductory exercise

Before looking at the passage below, answer these questions.

1 Which of these courses of study would be most helpful to you in order to qualify for each of these careers? Match each course of study on the left with one of the professions on the right.

Biology
Drama
Economics
Engineering
English
Mathematics
Modern Languages
Theology

Actor
Architect
Computer programmer
Economist
Interpreter
Journalist
Naturalist
Priest

2 What sort of experiments or research would you be likely to do if you were: *a* an archaeologist; *b* an astronomer; *c* a doctor; *d* a metallurgist; *e* a sociologist?

A career in the food industry

CAREERS INFORMATION SERVICE

DISTINGUISHING between margarine and butter may not be as difficult as the old advertisements used to claim. But
5 can you tell marge from ice-cream?

For scientists working in the food industry, this may be a more apposite question. Margarine and
10 ice-cream, as it happens, are both **emulsions** and chemists who specialise in this area may not distinguish much between them in their research. Their findings
15 about one of them in the laboratory can be applied also to the other – the **pure science** is the same. And when they are looking at production methods for such
20 foodstuffs, they will cooperate with engineers just like their opposite numbers in the petroleum or plastics industries.

emulsions: milky liquids with drops of oil or fat suspended in them

pure science: theoretical study of science. Applied science is for a practical purpose.

In other words, scientists in the
25 food industry remain basically chemists, or biochemists, or microbiologists or whatever. Today, they are working on tinned

spaghetti, but tomorrow, it could
30 be soapflakes.

From the careers angle, the
important feature of this is that
young scientists who are thinking
about entering the food industry
35 have no need to fear that they are
boxing themselves into a narrow
occupational area. On the
contrary, with most 'food'
employers there is an open door
40 into a diverse range of research
and other opportunities.

As a generalisation, it is fair to
say that scientists in this field are
employed in five main areas:
45 devising new products and
improving existing products;
devising new processes and
improving existing processes; and
finally, in dealing with 'external'
50 constraints and controls such as

meeting the requirements of new
EEC regulations.

In undertaking this work, a wide
range of **disciplines** is required.
55 However, by far the most popular
subject with employers and
recruiters is chemistry,
particularly where physical
chemistry has been the main
60 subject studied. Biochemists are
also well received, and chemical
engineers are needed to marry up
the work of the scientists to the
large-scale production processes.
65 Students who have taken degrees
in subjects like food science and
technology obviously enter the
industry as well, but, relatively
speaking, their numbers are not
70 large. In short, it is by no means
necessary to have specialised in the
subject while at college in order to
enter the industry on graduation.

EEC: European Economic
Community (Common Market)
discipline: here, subjects of
instruction

From *Food for Scientific Thought* by Edward Fennell in the
Daily Telegraph (abridged)

Exercise 1

*Compare each of these statements with the
passage and decide which are true and which
are false. **More than one** may be true in each
group.*

1   Scientists in the food industry
   a   cannot tell the difference between
       margarine and butter.
   b   cannot tell the difference between
       margarine and ice-cream.
   c   know that the last two are similar
       products.
2   In their profession, scientists in the food
   industry
   a   work with engineers.
   b   work with experts in the plastics industry.
   c   only work on foodstuffs.
3   Employment in the food industry may involve
   a   developing new products.
   b   changing old products.
   c   altering the composition of products for
       legal reasons.
4   Employers in the food industry are very
   interested in
   a   chemical engineers.
   b   experts in food technology.
   c   biochemists.

Exercise 2

*Decide which of the statements given express
the **main** points of the passage. Choose
between a and b in each case.*

1   The work of scientists in the food industry
   a   enables them to work on more than one
       product at the same time.
   b   is so widely applicable that their basic
       knowledge is more important than
       specialised expertise.
2   Consequently,
   a   opportunities for those with specialised
       knowledge of foodstuffs are more varied.
   b   there is little risk that they will be forced to
       limit themselves to one kind of research.
3   To attract employers, students should,
   therefore,
   a   have a good degree in a relevant
       scientific subject.
   b   take a degree in food science or
       technology.

Exercise 3

Find words or phrases in the passage that are similar in meaning to the following. The number in brackets indicates the paragraph where the word or phrase is to be found.

1 appropriate (2)
2 discoveries (2)
3 work together (2)
4 equivalents (2)
5 point of view (4)
6 enclosing (in) (4)
7 the opposite is true (4)
8 varied (4)
9 inventing (5)
10 outside (5)
11 limitations (5)
12 agreeing to do (6)
13 join (6)
14 comparatively (6)
15 in brief (6)
16 not at all (6)

Exercise 4

● **famous, favourable, favourite, popular**

Choose the correct word to complete the following.

Chemistry was my ¹_____ subject at school. We had a good teacher, who was ²_____ with all the students. When I applied for a job, he wrote a very ³_____ report about me. Since then, he has become a ⁴_____ scientist. His picture was in one of the ⁵_____ papers the other day.

Students' bank accounts

Some information about banks

Study the following information about banks and read the advertisement on the next page before attempting the exercises.

The main business of banks is to borrow money from customers and lend it to others at advantageous **interest rates**. If you have a **current account**, they will not pay you **interest** and in some cases you will have to pay **bank charges**; on the other hand, you can draw out the **cash on demand**. After all, it's your money! If you have a **deposit account**, you receive interest on condition that you leave the money in the bank for an agreed period of time. You must notify the bank in advance to withdraw money, though in practice this is not usually difficult. The bank charges **interest on loans** of money and **commission on services**, such as providing **travellers' cheques**.

At regular intervals, the bank sends you a **statement** of your **bank balance**. If it is **in credit** (**in the black**), the statement arrives on an agreed date; if it goes **into the red** and you owe the bank money, they normally advise you sooner!

You don't need a degree to see why more students hand us their grant cheques than any other bank.

In the last five years, more students have opened accounts with NatWest than any other bank.

Because we're the only bank to have worked out a really comprehensive service for young people moving on to further education.

YOUR OWN ACCOUNT BEFORE YOUR GRANT CHEQUE COMES THROUGH.

Did you know it can take a couple of weeks to set up a new bank account? So, if you wait till you arrive at college (even with a grant cheque in your pocket) there'd be some time before you could get your hands on the money.

By using the NatWest Student Grant Service the problem's solved.

Just tell us where you're hoping to study (see coupon) and we'll start to organise your account. Before you get to college, before you get your grant cheque. We'll locate the branch nearest your college and give them the details.

When you get to college, just present your first Local Education Authority grant cheque and you'll have your own account waiting for you.

And money to spend when you most need it.

MORE BRANCHES IN AND AROUND CAMPUS THAN ANY OTHER BANK.

NatWest has more branches than any other bank.

So, when you apply for your new account – especially if your college or university is a long way from home – you can be sure we'll find a branch on or near campus.

NO ACCOUNT CHARGE ON YOUR CURRENT ACCOUNT.

All we ask is that you keep your current account in credit. For that, we'll provide the complete current account service, including regular statements. without charging you for it, for as long as you remain a full-time student.

YOUR OWN CHEQUE CARD STRAIGHT AWAY.

Most new account holders are obliged to wait a few months before receiving a cheque card. The Student Grant Service does away with this delay and assuming you're 18 or over provides you with a cheque card as soon as your first L.E.A. grant cheque is paid into your current account.

A cheque card guarantees payment of cheques up to £50 and means you can draw cash from any branch in the country.

INSTANT CASH WITH THE NATWEST SERVICECARD.

Together with your cheque card, we'll give you a NatWest Servicecard. It means you can draw cash, up to an agreed limit, 24 hours a day, from any of our Servicetill machines throughout the country. By using the Servicetill you can also order an up-to-date statement, a new cheque book, and (during working hours) get an instant check on your bank balance.

NO COMMISSION TO PAY ON NATWEST TRAVEL CHEQUES.

With long holidays ahead, travel abroad could well be on your agenda.

If so, our Student Grant Service provides you with another benefit – we take no commission on any order for up to £200 worth of Natwest Travel Cheques and/or foreign currency in any one year for as long as you remain a student.

If you think we've made our case for the NatWest Student Grant Service, that it really does make money matters easier for students, then the easiest way to open an account would be to fill in the coupon and send it off FREEPOST. If there's more you'd like to know just drop in at any NatWest branch and ask all the questions you want.

NatWest Student Grant Service

Get this coupon to us (at least 14 days before your start date) and let the NatWest Student Grant Service take care of the rest

Mr Mrs Miss Ms (Surname) _____

(Other names) _____

Home Address _____

_____ Date of Birth _____

Name of University College _____

Course _____ Start date _____ Length of course _____

NatWest Services required (Tick box)
Servicecard (24hr cash) ☐   Cheque book and cheque card ☐   Deposit Savings account ☐

Signature _____

National Westminster Bank Limited. Student Grant Service. FREEPOST 41 Lothbury, London EC2B 2GN No stamp required

For an easier start to student life. STM2

(the information in this advertisement was correct as of June 1983)

Exercise 1

Choose the most likely meaning of these words in the context of the bank advertisement.

1 **grant** (line 7): **a** a loan from the bank **b** financial support from the local authority
2 **branch** (line 20): **a** a local office **b** part of a tree
3 **campus** (line 26): **a** a place to put up a tent **b** the university area
4 **up-to-date** (line 52): **a** modern and fashionable **b** accurate at the time
5 **benefit** (line 58): **a** profit **b** advantage
6 **drop in** (lines 66–7): **a** call **b** fall

Exercise 2

*Compare each of these statements with the advertisement and decide which are true and which are false. **More than one** may be true in each group.*

1 If you arrive at college with a cheque to pay for your living expenses, you can
    a cash it at any bank.
    b only cash it at the National Westminster.
    c cash it if you have a bank account there.
2 If you take advantage of the offer in the advertisement,
    a you can open a bank account without paying anything in advance.
    b the bank will lend you money.
    c the bank will provide you with money when you need it.
3 The National Westminster has branches
    a at every university.
    b near every university.
    c at more universities than other banks do.
4 You will not be charged by the bank if you
    a have an account.
    b do not owe it money.
    c are a full-time student.
5 You have a cheque card
    a if you are a student.
    b if you are over 18.
    c if you have paid in your grant cheque and are 18.
6 The cheque card allows you to draw
    a £50 at your own branch.
    b £50 at another branch.
    c £50 at any bank.
7 With a NatWest Service Card, you can *at any time*
    a find out what your present balance is.
    b obtain the latest statement of your balance.
    c get a new cheque book.
    d draw £50.
8 If you want to travel abroad, you can obtain, without charge, travel cheques to the value of
    a £200 at any time.
    b £200 in a year.
    c £150 in a year.
    d £150 at any time.
9 If you start your course on October 1st and want to take advantage of this offer, should you post the coupon by
    a September 15th?
    b September 20th?
    c September 25th?
10 If you plan to fill in the form, will you put a stamp on the envelope?

11 If you have got *all the answers right*, imagine you are a student with a grant and fill in the form. If not, check with another student!

Exercise 3

Find words or phrases in the advertisement that are similar in meaning to the following. The column, left or right, in which the word or phrase is to be found is indicated in brackets.
  1 arrives (left)
  2 establish (left)
  3 arrive at (left)
  4 find (left)
  5 forced (right)
  6 removes (right)
  7 provided that (right)
  8 take out money (right)
  9 immediate (right)
10 list of plans (right)
11 supplies (right)
12 look after (right)

Exercise 4

● arrive, get (to), reach

Study these examples.
e.g. When your grant cheque arrives/reaches **you**/gets **to you**, cash it.
    When you arrive **at**/reach/get **to** college, drop in on me.
    When you arrive **in**/reach/get **to** London, ring me up. (Preposition!)
    What time did you arrive/reach/get home last night? (No preposition)
    I can't **reach** it/It's **out of reach**/It's not **within reach**.
    When you arrive **at**/reach/get **to** my age, you'll understand.

Choose the correct verb and put it in the correct form to complete the following.
1 Has the train _____ yet?
2 Have they _____ the top of the hill yet?
3 The plane finally _____ to New York five hours late.
4 Your letter didn't _____ me in time.
5 When you _____ to 70, you often feel tired.
6 Has the train _____ at the station yet?

Cars

11

Introductory exercise

A number of common words are different in
British and American English usage.

*Find the British English equivalent on the right
for the American English word on the left.*

apartment	fall	autumn	petrol
automobile	gas (gasoline)	film	rubber
candy	movie	flat	sweets
elevator	pants	lift	term
eraser	semester	(motor)car	trousers

A very lucky driver

When I got an automobile of my own and began to drive it, I
brought to the enterprise a magnificent ignorance of the workings
of a gas engine, and a profound disinterest in its oily secrets. On
several occasions, worried friends of an engineering turn of mind
5 attempted to explain the nature of gas engines to me, but they
succeeded only in losing me in a mechanical maze of terminology.
I developed the notion that the gas engine was more soundly
constructed than I was. I elaborate this point only to show you on
what unequal terms the motor car and I were brought together.
10   Out of my long and dogged bouts with automobiles of various
makes, there comes back to me now only one truly pleasurable
experience. There may have been others, but I doubt it. I was
driving in the British Isles in 1938, and came one day to a sudden,
coughing stop in a far and lonely section of Scotland. The car had
15 run out of gas in the wilderness. This car's gasoline gauge had a
trick of mounting toward 'Full' instead of sinking toward 'Empty'
when the tank was running low, one of many examples of pure
cussedness of which it was capable. There I was, miles from any
village, with not even a farmhouse in sight. On my left was a thick
20 wood, out of which the figure of a man suddenly appeared. He
asked me what was the matter, and I said I had run out of petrol. 'It
just happens,' he told me, 'that I have a can of petrol.' With that,
he went back into the woods, and came out again with a **five-gallon
can** of gasoline. He put it in the tank for me, I thanked him, paid
25 for it, and drove on.
     Once when I was telling this true but admittedly remarkable
story, at a party in New York, a bright-eyed young woman
exclaimed, 'But when the man emerged from the lonely woods,

cussedness: awkwardness
(UK)

five-gallon can:
gallons = approximately
22.5 litres

vanish: disappear (by magic)

miles away from any village, far from the nearest farmhouse,
30 carrying a five-gallon can of gasoline, why didn't you ask him how
he happened to be there with it?' I lighted a cigarette. 'Madam,' I
said, 'I was afraid he would **vanish.**' She gave a small laugh and
moved away from me. Everybody always does.

From *The Thurber Carnival* by James Thurber

Exercise 1

Choose the most likely meaning of these words in the context of the passage. Refer to the hints given in brackets if you are not sure of the answers.

1 **enterprise** (line 2): *a* factory *b* undertaking (Driving a car?)
2 **disinterest** (line 3): *a* lack of interest *b* selfishness (Ignorance?)
3 **maze** (line 6): a state of *a* admiration *b* confusion (Losing me?)
4 **soundly** (line 7): refers to *a* noise *b* reliability (Constructed?)
5 **elaborate** (line 8): *a* complicated *b* explain at length (Grammar?)
6 **dogged** (line 10): *a* implies determination *b* relates to dogs (Dogs!?)
7 **bouts** (line 10): *a* struggles *b* journeys (Unequal terms?)
8 **wilderness** (line 15): is land that is *a* cultivated *b* uncultivated (Farm?)
9 What are a **gauge** (line 15) and a **tank** (line 17) used for, judging from the passage?

Exercise 2

Understanding humour often depends on recognising that the adjective and the noun are not usually seen together, or the combination may be normal but in the context suggests the writer had other ideas.

Answer these questions on the passage.

1 What is strange about **magnificent ignorance**?
2 Why is it unusual to show **a profound disinterest**?
3 What is funny about saying **the gas engine was more soundly constructed than I was**?

4 What sort of relationship between man and car is suggested by **trick of mounting toward 'Full'** and **pure cussedness**?
5 Why do we get the idea that the writer did not respond in a usual way to the **bright-eyed young woman**?
6 What reaction is suggested by **a small laugh**?

Exercise 3

Answer these questions on the passage.

1 How do we know that
   a the writer knows nothing about cars mechanically?
   b does not enjoy driving?
   c is used to people thinking he is mad?
2 Which do you think is the point of the story? The writer
   a was so absent-minded that he wasn't surprised by what happened.
   b wanted to show that coincidences are always possible.
   c thought it might be a miracle and didn't want to risk spoiling it.

Exercise 4

● **A**   **achieve, manage (to), realise, succeed (in)**

*Use each verb, **at least once**, in the correct form to complete the following.*
A friend of mine taught me to drive but it was a long time before I ¹_____ in handling the car with confidence. My friend tried to explain how cars worked but never ²_____. All he ³_____ was to confuse me even more. Now that I ⁴_____ how little I understood them, it seems wonderful that I ⁵_____ to pass the test.

45

● B afraid, ashamed, responsible, sorry, worried

Choose the correct word to complete the following.

I had a slight accident the other day. I was passing a parked car in a narrow street and I scratched the paintwork. Then the driver came up.

'I'm terribly ¹_____,' I said.

'Drivers like you ought to be ²_____ of yourselves,' he said. He was very angry.

'I know I'm ³_____ for what happened,' I said, 'and I'll pay for the damage.'

I was rather ⁴_____ of him. He was much bigger than me.

He still looked very ⁵_____. 'It's my father's car, you see.' he said.

I felt ⁶_____ for him. 'I'm ⁷_____ I can't come with you to explain,' I said, 'but I'll give you my name and address, of course.'

● C brand, class, make, model, trademark

Choose the correct word to complete the following.

A: What ¹_____ is your car?

B: It's a Ford, the latest ²_____.

A: Which ³_____ of coffee do you prefer?

B: Bear ⁴_____. That's the one with the teddy bear as a ⁵_____. The others aren't in the same ⁶_____.

● D bring, carry, fetch, take

bring (= from there to here), **take** (= from here to there), **fetch** means to go and bring/get, **carry** means move from one place to another, with the weight of something being held.

*Use each verb, **at least once**, in the correct form to complete the following.*

1 He went into the woods and came back, _____ a can of petrol in his hand.
   'I've _____ you some petrol,' he said.

2 He _____ the can from me. 'I'll _____ you some petrol,' he said.

3 I've forgotten to _____ my books to class. I left them at home.

4 Mother probably _____ your slippers upstairs, Grandad. Shall I _____ them for you?

5 This soup is cold. _____ it away and _____ me some fruit juice.

The Cinema

Introductory exercise

*Before looking at the passage below, answer
these questions.*

1 Can you name: **a** a film comedy; **b** a historical
film; **c** a horror film; **d** a musical; **e** a romantic
drama; **f** a science fiction film; **g** a socially committed film; **h** a thriller; **i** a western; **j** a war
film?
2 Do you remember the names of: **a** the stars;
b the characters they played; **c** the directors?

Hollywood musicals

People seem either to adore musicals or detest them, and logic will not sway
their opinions on this not-too-crucial issue. People either go to the movies to
be entertained and to escape reality, or else they go to be engaged by
themes and to be moved by art. To the first group (a vast majority), musicals
are the ***raison d'être*** of the cinema, and to the second they are evidence
of its debasement. Of course, both groups are wrong.

It is important to give musicals their due and to honour them in
proportion to their worth. Some bridge the gap by claiming that Europeans
are best at making art films, and that Americans are **preeminent** in
escapist **genres**. Hollywood was a dream factory, their argument goes,
and its greatest products were escapist fantasies: thrillers, westerns,
musicals.

Though this position is much too doctrinaire, and has a patronising air
about it, one must risk the wrath of the musical **cultists** and say that it
comes fairly close to the truth. Musicals are the most escapist of genres, and
Americans seem to be most excellent at making them. This may be
accounted for by the size of the country and its traditions, the quality and
diversity of American song-writing and of its singing and dancing
entertainers, plus the reservoir of material and people provided by the
musical stage. And though the Hollywood studio system had many defects,
most of them deriving from the fact that movie-making was considered
above all else a business, no one can deny Hollywood's technical expertise,
the craftsmanship and inventiveness of its **artisans**, and the respective
sizes of its budgets and sound stages. Combine American talents, American
expertise, American budgets, and a desire to manufacture an escapist
product, and you come up with a peculiarly American genre, perhaps not an
art form, but an entertainment form that must be admired.

From *The Great Movies*
by William Bayer

raison d'être: justification for the
existence of
pre-eminent: very distinguished,
outstanding

genres: forms of art
cultists: those who have made
them almost like a religion
artisans: craftsmen

Exercise 1

Study the context to decide the meaning of the following words and phrases, using the suggestions given to guide you.

1 **engaged by ... moved by** (lines 3–4): A contrast is intended here. We respond to films with minds and hearts. Which phrase suggests intellectual involvement, which an emotional response?
2 **give musicals their due** (line 7): What is due is what they deserve. How else could we say this? — **be _____ to musicals.**
3 **bridge the gap** (line 8): What is a **gap**? Why do you think we talk about **bridging** a gap? What is the gap referred to here?
4 The attitude referred to in the second paragraph is **doctrinaire** (line 13) and **patronising** (line 13). It involves a neat simplification, and also says Hollywood only produces fantasies. What sort of critic is likely to have these attitudes towards Hollywood?
5 A **reservoir** is usually a place where water is stored for a town. What could it mean here (line 19) in relation to material and people?
6 **budgets and sound stages** (line 24): What could the money available for films and the studios where they were made in Hollywood have in common?

Exercise 2

Answer these questions on the passage in short sentences.

1 Why do people react strongly for or against musicals?
2 Why are musicals the 'raison d'être of the cinema' for some people?
3 Why does the writer disagree with extreme points of view about musicals?
4 How do some critics explain Hollywood's success with some genres?
5 Does the writer agree on the whole with these critics?
6 What are the *main* reasons he gives for the success of Hollywood musicals?

Exercise 3

*Compare each of these statements with the passage and decide which are true and which are false. **More than one** may be true in each group. Pay particular attention to the use of words like **everyone, only, mainly.***

1 a Everyone enjoys musicals.
   b Most people enjoy musicals.
   c Some people despise them.
   d A lot of people despise them. (A lot?)
2 Most people enjoy musicals, *according to the passage* (and never mind your own personal opinion!) because they are
   a entertaining.
   b unreal.
   c illogical.
   d fantasies.
3 The writer thinks musicals are
   a fantasies.
   b escapist.
   c always excellent.
   d a valid form of cinema.
4 The success of Hollywood musicals can be attributed mainly to
   a the studio system.
   b the singers.
   c a variety of factors.
   d a love of escapism.

Exercise 4

Find words or phrases in the passage that are similar in meaning to the following. The number in brackets indicates the paragraph where the word or phrase is to be found.

1 love (*v.*) (1)
2 hate (*v.*) (1)
3 influence (*v.*) (1)
4 low standards (1)
5 value (*n.*) (2)
6 anger (*n.*) (3)
7 explained (3)
8 resulting (3)
9 wish (*n.*) (3)
10 produce as a result (3)

Exercise 5

● **cost** (*v.*), **expense(s)**, **price**, **value** (*n.*), **worth** (*adj. and n.*)

Study these examples.

e.g. The **cost** of production was enormous. It **cost** millions of dollars.

We must save him **at all costs** (= whatever the sacrifice).

He has backed the film **at considerable personal expense/cost.**

He is paid **expenses**, as well as a salary.

What's the **price?** (How much must I pay? What does it **cost?**)

The **value** of the pound has fallen. (Its international buying power)

Your work has been **of great value** to me. (Very useful)

This ring **has** great **value** to me personally. It is also **worth** a lot of money, but I would never sell it.

How much is it **worth?** (Real value or, more often, in money)

Is it **worth doing?** (Is there any point in doing it?)

The **true worth** (= artistic value) of these films is doubtful.

Use the words and forms given above to complete the following.

In the great days of Hollywood, films were often made at enormous ¹_____, with no thought of their artistic ²_____. The ³_____ of production was so high because of the star system. Producers did not ask: 'Is the film ⁴_____ making?' but 'How much will it ⁵_____?' Sometimes they were prepared to get an actress's services at all ⁶_____, even if it meant paying her mother's ⁷_____ to travel with her. The ⁸_____ they paid was irrelevant. The question 'How much is her performance ⁹_____ to the film?' was not connected with acting, but with the box office. Stars were paid millions of dollars, at a time when the ¹⁰_____ of the dollar was much less that it is now. Their films were not of great ¹¹_____, and it is hard to estimate their true ¹²_____, because good technique was linked to superficial stories. That's the ¹³_____ one pays for commercialism.

NOTE: an **expensive** dinner, a **valuable** painting (worth a lot of money), a **valuable** man (useful), **precious** stones (e.g. diamonds), **precious** memories (of emotional value), **worthy of** consideration (= worth considering).
Priceless, invaluable = enormously valuable, **valueless, worthless** = without value, **inexpensive** = cheap.

Lexical Progress Test 2

You must choose the word or phrase which best completes each sentence. For each question, 1 to 25, indicate the correct answer, A, B, C or D. The time for the test is 20 minutes.

1 You need a good, _____ pair of boots for mountain climbing.
   A rough B rude C rusty D tough

2 You'll have to go through customs when you cross the French _____.
   A border B boundary C edge D line

3 You'll see it straight in front of you when you turn the corner. You can't _____ it!
   A fail B loose C lose D miss

4 If you're looking for video equipment, I _____ you to go to Brown's.
   A propose B recommend C refer D suggest

5 She's very _____ to criticism, and easily upset.
   A senseless B sensible C sensitive D sentimental

6 She took an umbrella with her, to _____ getting wet.
   A avoid B deny C prevent D resist

7 Luckily, she wasn't _____ injured in the accident.
   A seriously B slightly C strictly D strongly

8 Living abroad and enjoying it depends on getting used to the _____ of the country.
   A customs B habits C programmes D uses

9 Why are you accusing me? It wasn't my _____!
   A blame B fail C fault D guilt

10 I told her to go away, but she _____ on seeing you.
    A claims B demands C insists D requires

11 Ideas like that are out of _____ these days.
    A date B mind C mood D time

12 Her first song was a hit and she's been very _____ ever since.
    A favourite B known C preferred D popular

13 Have you _____ the tickets for the theatre tomorrow?
    A booked B engaged C paid D preserved

14 He _____ to pass the examination at the second attempt.
    A achieved B managed C realised D succeeded

15 He _____ us how to operate the machine.
    A described B explained C instructed D taught

16 I shouldn't have treated him so badly. I feel _____ of myself.
    A ashamed B responsible C sorry D worried

17 I couldn't concentrate on my work with all that noise. It _____ me _____.
    A broke...down B put...off C sent...on D turned...off

18 Do you like my new car? It's the latest _____.
    A brand B mark C model D pattern

19 I can't _____ people singing out of tune.
    A hold B pass C stand D support

20 The clock _____ twelve, and we all raised our glasses.
    A beat B hit C shot D struck

21 The _____ of the pound has fallen recently.
    A expense B price C value D worth

22 He's got a much better _____ now, in an advertising agency.
    A duty B employment C job D work

23 _____ to write to Aunt Mary to thank her for her present.
    A Refer B Remember C Remind D Repeat

24 He's always nervous when he has to make a _____.
    A discussion B pronunciation C speech D talk

25 If you expect children to be polite, you must _____ them up properly.
    A bring B grow C rise D take

50

Illness

Introductory exercise

Before looking at the passage below, answer these questions.

1 Have you had any of the following: a cold, flu, measles, mumps, rheumatism? Describe the symptoms (what you felt).

2 Which of the following would you call serious, and which are infectious: **a** chickenpox; **b** pneumonia; **c** smallpox; **d** stomachache; **e** tonsilitis?

Health insurance

It isn't until you or someone close to you is in hospital that you realise how expensive it is – even when all the medical expenses are paid. There are so many 'extras' you hadn't thought of.

It's so much worse when someone is in hospital for a really serious illness. Take, for example, a heart attack. It's not unusual for a patient to be in hospital for a month – or even longer.

That's why you need the new Lloyd's Life Hospital Cash Plan. It is specially designed to protect you and your family against the financial disaster of a serious illness that requires a long spell in hospital. And the cost of this protection can be as low as £2.95 a month.

Your hospital cash benefits begin from your first day in hospital due to accident and from your eighth day due to illness. Lloyd's Life is primarily concerned that your Hospital Cash Plan will be there to meet the heavy financial strain of a long hospital stay in case of serious illness or injury.

Your cash benefits are paid directly to you – not to a doctor or a hospital.

Also, these cash benefits are paid in addition to any benefits you may receive from National Insurance or any other insurance . . . regardless of the actual amount of your hospital bill. And your benefits are all *tax-free* for at least one year thanks to a current Inland Revenue concession!

No medical examination is required and no health questions are asked when you enrol. You cannot be refused this Hospital Cash Plan if you are over age 18 and under 65.

Because different individuals and families have different budgets and different needs for hospital cash protection, you have two plans from which to choose. You may also choose to include your spouse and/or your children. In fact, we suggest that you include your entire family since hospitalisation is a family matter, and it is financially unsettling when any family member goes into hospital.

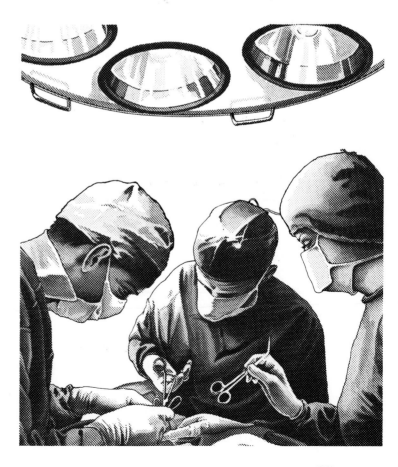

40   In order that your rates can be kept as low as possible, hospital stays due to certain specified causes are understandably not covered. These are clearly detailed in your Policy Document. Illnesses or injuries for which you received advice or treatment
45 during the two years before your policy was issued will not be covered for the first two years your policy is in effect.

    All other conditions are covered. And, in addition, after your policy has been in effect for two years, you
50 are even covered for all pre-existing illnesses and injuries.

    Lloyd's Life Assurance Limited is the insurance company formed by Lloyd's of London, probably the best-known insurance institution in the world.
55 Lloyd's Life developed the Hospital Cash Plan after extensive research into the needs of men and women for low-cost supplementary hospital insurance and it is brought to you by S A I Services (UK) Ltd.

Lloyd's life

Lloyd's Life Hospital Cash Plan Administrator,
SAI House, 349 London Road, Camberley, Surrey GU15 3HQ

You pay only £1 for your first month's cover...
...so the more cover you choose, the more money you save.

			AGE at last birthday				
PLAN A	Monthly*						
pays you **£115.50 a week**...	Premiums for	18-34	35-44	45-49	50-54	55-59	60-64***
over **£500 a month**...	Individual only	£2.95	£3.75	£4.45	£5.15	£6.15	£7.95
up to **£6,022.50** for each	Individual & spouse**	£4.90	£6.50	£7.90	£9.30	£11.30	£14.90
covered stay in hospital							
	Each dependent child age 2 to 17...£1.15***						
PLAN B	Individual only	£4.90	£6.50	£7.90	£9.30	£11.30	£14.90
	Individual & spouse**	£8.80	£12.00	£14.80	£17.60	£21.60	£28.80
pays you **£231 a week**...	Each dependent child age 2 to 17....£2.30***						
over **£1,000 a month**...							
up to **£12,045** for each	* Monthly premiums are payable only by Direct Debiting Mandate.						
covered stay in hospital	** Where both husband and wife are insured, premiums are based on age of the older spouse, at the time the Plan goes into effect.						
	*** Benefits are halved at age 65 and for dependent children.						

Notes:
1. No person may be insured under more than one Lloyd's Life Hospital Cash Plan.
2. For the first five years, your premiums are guaranteed not to increase unless there is a general adjustment to all policies of this type.

Direct Debiting Mandate: an instruction to the bank to pay a sum on the given date at regular intervals

---

Exercise 1

Choose the most likely meaning of these words in the context of the passage.

1 **extras** (line 4): *a* other people *b* additional expenses
2 **spell** (line 12): relates to *a* language *b* time
3 **strain** (line 18): relates to *a* muscles *b* financial difficulties

4 **Inland Revenue** (lines 26–7): *a* a tax office *b* hospital administration
5 **spouse** (line 35): *a* wife *b* husband or wife

Exercise 2

Read the information about these two people and answer the questions below. Answer yes/no or give figures for monthly payment for both Sally and Bill.

SALLY OWEN, 24, single. She was in a car crash four days ago. She pays National Insurance. She enrolled for herself a year ago.

BILL COLLINS, 49, married. He had a heart attack six days ago. He pays National Insurance and his firm also insures him. He enrolled himself, his wife, Mary, 46, and three children aged 14, 7 and 5, three years ago.

1   Is he/she receiving benefit?
2   Is it paid to him/her directly?
3   Does other insurance affect benefit paid?
4   Does he/she have to pay tax on it?
5   Did he/she pass a medical examination for acceptance?
6   Did he/she have to answer questions about health?
7   How much is he/she paying a month for insurance here?

Exercise 3

The following people are interested in the Plan. Read the data about them and then compare it with the information given in the advertisement to answer the questions.

JANE LORD, 17. For herself. She is in good health.

JACK CUMMINS, 33. For himself, his wife, Joan, 35, and their children aged 6 and 1. They are all in good health.

WALTER SMART, 55. For himself and his wife, Alice, 47. He had a heart attack a year ago and is still receiving treatment.

JENNY WILSON, 34. For herself and her daughter, aged 12. She has back trouble and went to see the doctor about it last week.

1   Is he/she eligible? If not, why not?
2   Will he/she receive benefit on the same terms as Sally and Bill? Will members of the family receive benefit on the same terms in all cases? If not, why not, in each case?
3   How much will he/she have to pay: **a** the first month; **b** the month after that?

Exercise 4

● **A   ache, disease, harm, illness, pain**

Choose the correct word to complete the following. Use plural forms where appropriate.

1   stomach _____
2   a _____ in the chest
3   ear _____
4   tooth _____
5   a sharp _____ in my leg
6   a head _____
7   an infectious _____
8   He has just recovered from a serious _____.
9   These tablets won't do you any _____.
10   He is an expert on tropical _____, like malaria.
11   There is no _____ in taking aspirins for a head _____, but you should not take antibiotics without a doctor's prescription.
12   When I burnt my hand the _____ was unbearable, and even now I still feel a dull _____ sometimes.

● **B   heal, improve, recover**

Use each verb in the correct form to complete the following.

His condition has [1]_____ since yesterday. The wound has [2]_____ and his temperature has gone down. In a few days, he will have [3]_____ completely.

● **C   blow, crash, flash, shock**

Choose the correct word to complete the following.

There was a sudden [1]_____ of lightning. He felt a [2]_____ on his head, and fell to the ground. He was standing under a tree and it hit him as it fell. The main problem he is suffering from now is the effect of [3]_____ on his nervous system. The other patient in the next bed was in a car [4]_____, and the one over there touched an electric wire and got a severe [5]_____, with burns.

Shopping

14

Introductory exercise

Before looking at the passage, answer these questions.

1 Which of the following are fruit and which are vegetables?

apple	celery	onion	pineapple
banana	cherry	orange	plum
bean	lemon	pea	potato
cabbage	lettuce	peach	strawberry
carrot	marrow	pear	tomato

2 What sort of food would you: ***a*** boil; ***b*** fry; ***c*** grill; ***d*** roast; ***e*** stew?

3 What sort of food could you: ***a*** chop; ***b*** melt; ***c*** peel; ***d*** slice; ***e*** stir? And why would you do these things?

Fruit and vegetables

cloves: a spice used in cooking, often to add to the flavour of apples

The best place to brighten dull January days is the greengrocer's or supermarkets with their vast colourful counters of fruit and
5 vegetables from every corner of the world.

Never has there been so much choice in exotic fruits in the middle of winter.
10 A nutritious meal need not necessarily be cooked and long slaved over to be appetising, and with current supplies of fresh fruit and vegetables and mild
15 temperatures, cold tables are a particularly attractive possibility.

Avocados are cheap and plentiful – as little as 25p each –
20 although they need 'dressing-up' they can make interesting eating.

Prawns and a rich dressing are complementary, but try a much cheaper avocado recipe using
25 lightly grilled strips of smoked bacon, lettuce, and finely slice the avocado and serve with a vinaigrette dressing.

Another increasingly popular
30 vegetable is the French bean. Although they are £1 per pound

they are full of protein and go a long way. Try cooking them with onions, garlic and canned
35 tomatoes or as a straight main vegetable with a bacon joint.

Although there is little evidence of a reduction in the price of sliced bacon yet, bacon
40 joints are slightly down in price.

Both bacon and pork have extra tang cooked with fruit. Bacon joints can be boiled with apples and **cloves**.
45 Excellent quality Cox's apples average 25p to 40p per pound although they are selling in the street markets for as little as 35p for two pounds. Try serving the
50 bacon with fresh pineapple. There are lots of small ripe ones to be had for about 60p each.

From *Dull Days Countered by Fruit* by Brenda Parry in the *Daily Telegraph*

Exercise 1

Choose the most likely meaning of these words in the context of the passage.

1 **exotic** (line 8): *a* tropical *b* foreign and unusual
2 **nutritious, appetising** (lines 10, 12): Which refers to *a* food value? *b* taste?
3 **slaved over** (line 12): When would someone have to work like a slave?
4 **dressing up** (line 20): *a* to be served with other food *b* decorating
5 **complementary** (line 23): *a* likely to produce compliments for the cook *b* a natural accompaniment (Look at the spelling.)
6 **tang** (line 42): refers to *a* flavour *b* nourishment
7 **Cox's** (line 45): a kind of *a* apple *b* pineapple

Exercise 2

*In this comprehension exercise, for the first time, you must choose **one** correct answer from three possibilities. Decide by comparing each statement (true/false) with the text. Find reasons in each case to explain why the wrong answers are wrong.*

1 The advantage of fruit and vegetable dishes is that
  a they come from all over the world.
  b they are colourful.
  c they do not require much hard work in cooking.
2 Cold meals are particularly attractive this January because
  a they do not require much hard work in cooking.
  b they are cheap.
  c the weather is warmer than usual.
3 Avocados
  a are interesting if served with something else.
  b are preferable on their own.
  c taste better with bacon than with prawns.
4 French beans
  a are always sent long distances.
  b should always be served with other vegetables.
  c are not quite as expensive as they seem.

5 Cox's apples
  a taste better with bacon.
  b cost less in street markets.
  c can be bought for 60p each.

Exercise 3

Find words or phrases in the passage that mean the opposite of the following. The words are given in the order in which they appear in the passage.

1 worst
2 bright
3 tiny
4 dear
5 scarce
6 roughly
7 lacking (in)
8 increase

Buying a goldfish

Sue Arnold

'Just a goldfish,' I said. 'And a bowl, of course.'

'No bowls,' said the young man. 'We do fish tanks from £5.75 to £300.'

5 'Why no bowls?' I said. Even the £5.75 tank looked as if it could accommodate a **barracuda** in comfort.

'We had a fish expert along who said goldfish got very bored just swimming 10 round and round all day long,' said the young man. 'With a tank you can introduce a variety of eye-catching features in every corner – a coral arrangement perhaps or some 15 interesting shells.'

'How much would the cheapest goldfish tank cost?' I asked 'It's only a birthday present for a seven-year-old.'

The young man smiled politely. 20 'Well, let's see now. You could get a reasonable goldfish for £1.50, then the tank £5.75, then you'd need a couple of scoops of gravel for the bottom, £1, two coral branches, say £2, a selection of 25 shells, a water purifier and some fish food and conditioner. Shall we say £12 the lot?'

'Tell me honestly,' I said. 'Do you think a goldfish is worth £12? I know it 30 was aeons ago, but I can remember winning a goldfish at a fair for sixpence, and it lasted three years.'

The young man thought about it. 'For a seven-year-old? Frankly, no.' 35 He ruminated further. 'He'd get a kick out of the novelty for a week or so, but remember the fish have to be cleaned out every other day, and for a child that can be a drag. Besides, goldfish are 40 basically uninteresting creatures.'

We were standing alongside one of the £300 tanks. About 30 tiny **iridescent** fish, were zapping about.

'What about that sort of thing?' I 45 said.

'They're tropical fish. Beautiful, but troublesome,' said the young man.

'The water has to be kept at a constant temperature, the light has to 50 be regulated and you have to know which breed gets on with which, because some tropical fish eat others, Those, for example, eat those.'

'What are those?' I said, pointing to 55 the cannibals.

'They're £2.25 each,' he said. 'Golden somethings. Anyway, the £2.25 ones eat the 80p ones.'

It seemed fair.

60 'Just say I steer clear of fish altogether,' I said. 'How about a bird?'

barracuda: a very large fish

iridescent: changing colour because of the effect of light

From *Creature Comforts* by Sue Arnold in the *Observer Magazine* (abridged)

Exercise 1

Answer these questions on the passage.

1 Why was the writer surprised there were no bowls? (Two answers.)
2 And why were there no bowls?
3 Why did the writer wonder whether it was worth paying £12 for a goldfish? (Two answers.)
4 What was the salesman's opinion, and why?
5 Why do you have to know 'which breed gets on with which' if you buy tropical fish?
6 What did the writer think was 'fair', and why?

Exercise 2

Decide on the probable meaning of these words in the context of the passage.

1 **shells** (line 15): *a* eggshells *b* seashells
2 **scoops** (line 23): *a* weights *b* measures
3 **gravel** (line 23): *a* plants *b* stones
4 **aeons** (line 30): *a* months *b* ages
5 **ruminated … further** (line 35): What was he doing before this?
6 **a kick** (line 35): No, he wouldn't kick it, of course. Child's reaction?
7 **a drag** (line 39): a thrill? Not really — cleaning out a tank?
8 **zapping** (line 43): obviously what little fish do most of the time.
9 **steer clear of** (line 60): Note the writer's next question.

Exercise 3

● **A   beat, earn, gain, win**

*Use each verb, **at least once**, in the correct form to complete the following.*

1 We _____ the match yesterday. We _____ Arsenal 3–1.
2 My watch is fast. It has _____ ten minutes since yesterday.
3 The job itself is not very interesting and I don't _____ much money, but I've taken it to _____ experience.
4 The baby has _____ two kilos since we weighed him last.
5 Nowadays, teachers don't _____ children if they don't learn their lessons. Under the old system, a few _____ prizes but most hated school for the rest of their lives.
6 You're old enough now to _____ your own living.
7 The drummer accompanying the pop group was _____ the time.
8 He isn't really going to pay you. He's making excuses to _____ time.

● **B   base, basis, bottom, ground**

Choose the correct word to complete the following.

1 She lives at the _____ of the hill. The _____ there is very sandy and I don't think the house is built on a firm _____.
2 What's the _____ of his argument?
3 The water is quite shallow here. My feet are touching the _____.
4 When she saw the dead fly at the _____ of the cup, she dropped it, and it fell to the _____.

● **C   bored, boring, tired, tiring**

Choose the correct word to complete the following.

1 I'm so _____.
   — Of course, working hard in the garden is _____.

2 Put the television on if you're _____.
   — I'm not going to watch that _____ programme.

Education

Introductory exercise

Students often misunderstand passages, especially if they are on controversial subjects, because they form a preconceived idea of the writer's opinions after a few sentences.

After reading the first paragraph of this passage decide whether the following are true or false before reading on.

The study

a criticises teachers because they are fashionable.

b thinks Jamaican creole forms and cockney accents should be prohibited in the classroom.

c accuses teachers of deliberately trying to limit the political potential of minorities.

Varieties of English

Trendy teachers who refuse to teach working-class and immigrant children the forms of standard English because they believe Jamaican creole or cockney will do just as well are 'politically **emasculating**' their charges, says a study published today.

5   Mr **Arthur Scargill** would never have become powerful outside his native patch of Yorkshire without mastering standard English grammar, Prof. John Honey argues in *The Language Trap*.

    The rest of the country would not understand him, he says. He would have been without the rhetorical tools of his trade, and

10 people would have laughed at him for putting things quaintly.

    Mr Scargill was lucky, Prof. Honey says, because his father taught him that his life depended on his ability to handle words. Yet influential linguistic theorists using 'a travesty of scientific method' had seen to it that Britain was already embarking on a

15 course that had brought disaster in America.

    The theorists claimed that all non-standard forms of English were 'as good as' standard English, and should be taught in the schools. Prof. Honey notes that in American schools the attempt to teach so-called Black English had brought an outcry from black

20 parents, who mistrusted the motives of the teachers.

    The professor accuses researchers of rigging their experiments in order to show that Black English, or cockney or a West Country dialect is just as 'flexible, detailed and subtle' as standard English, if not more so.

25   Parents, however, tend not to agree that cockney is as good or useful to their offspring as the standard English version which would be understood all over this country and America.

Prof. Honey says that it is not necessary to lose a regional accent, but it is important to use standard grammatical forms.

30 'For schools to foster non-standard varieties of English is to place their pupils in a trap,' the professor writes. 'To persuade such speakers that their particular non-standard variety of English is in no way inferior, but simply different, is to play a cruel trick.'

trendy: trying to keep up with the latest fashion
emasculating: here, depriving them of strength, influence
Arthur Scargill: leader of the miners' Union

From *Creole and Cockney 'is 'ardly English'* by Margot Norman in the *Daily Telegraph* (abridged)

(The answer to the question at the beginning is that none of them are true.)

Exercise 1

Choose the most likely meaning of these words or phrases in the context of the passage.
1 **charges** (line 4): *a* costs *b* students (In charge of?)
2 **tools of his trade** (line 9): *a* the effective use of discourse in argument *b* a miner's pick and shovel
3 **quaintly** (line 10): *a* in an aggressive way *b* in an odd, amusing way
4 **travesty** (line 13): *a* system *b* distortion
5 **embarking** (line 14): *a* starting out *b* ending (what is the origin of 'embark'?)
6 **outcry** (line 19): *a* revolution *b* loud complaint (They 'cry out'.)
7 **rigging** (line 21): *a* planning efficiently *b* manipulating the results of
8 **offspring** (line 26): *a* children *b* production
9 **foster** (line 30): *a* encourage and promote *b* discourage and prevent

Exercise 2

*Compare each of these statements with the passage and decide which are true and which are false. **More than one** may be true in each group.*

1 Arthur Scargill would not have become a successful leader, in the professor's opinion, if he had not
   a come from Yorkshire.
   b dropped his Yorkshire accent.
   c learnt to speak grammatically.
2 This is because people would have
   a objected to his accent.
   b realised he was working-class.
   c been so amused that they would not have listened to him with complete attention.
3 Black people objected to Black English being taught because they
   a knew it was inferior.
   b wanted their children to sound like white people.
   c suspected that teachers wanted to keep them in a situation of social inferiority.
4 Parents do not agree with the theorists because
   a the experiments were badly organised.
   b they want their children to be understood everywhere.
   c they are snobbish in their attitudes.

Exercise 3

Decide which of the following arguments are put forward in the study.
1 It is necessary to have a standard English accent to succeed.
2 Standard English forms are more useful than variants that are not grammatical.
3 Teachers who deliberately prevent students from learning standard English forms are doing them harm politically.
4 Theorists mislead students by flattering them that their dialect is as widely acceptable as standard English.

5 Schools encouraging non-standard forms do so to trick students.
6 Immigrant and regional political leaders must be able to speak grammatically to have an effect on the country as a whole.
7 Non-standard forms are not as flexible as the standard form.
8 Working-class parents agree that regional or immigrant forms of language should be kept out of the classroom.

Exercise 4

Decide which statement in each group best summarises the aims of the study.
1 It is written as an attack on:
  a non-standard forms of English.
  b inaccurate scientific research.
  c teachers and theorists who prefer their own social attitudes to fact.
2 It argues that such non-standard forms as cockney are inferior because they
  a are working-class.
  b are not widely understood.
  c sound funny.
3 The article therefore discourages
  a non-standard grammar.
  b non-standard accents.
  c minority languages (e.g. Welsh).

Exercise 5

● A   accept, admit, agree, approve

*Use each verb, **at least once**, in the correct form to complete the following.*
A: I'm glad you have ¹_____ our invitation and ²_____ to speak to the teachers. I hope you realise that a lot of them don't ³_____ with you.
B: Oh, yes, I ⁴_____ that. In fact, I ⁵_____ that my arguments could be used for racial ends. But I am only interested in getting people to ⁶_____ on the need to teach standard forms. Obviously, I don't ⁷_____ of a policy that makes people feel inferior or say we shouldn't ⁸_____ people to jobs if they use non-standard forms. What worries me is that some people refuse to ⁹_____ that these forms are not widely used, publish misleading research and will not ¹⁰_____ their mistakes even when they are shown to be wrong.

● B   track, trap, trick, trip (*n. and v.*)

Choose the correct word to complete the following.
1 The police set a _____ for the thief, and he was caught.
2 He had got the money by a _____.
3 He went on a day-_____ to France.
4 He followed the animal's _____s in the snow. Suddenly, he _____ over a branch and fell into a _____ someone else had set.

Adventure

Introductory exercise

Before looking at the passage below, answer these questions.

1 Where would you be likely to see the following ships or boats and what are they usually used for? **a** a barge; **b** a cargo boat; **c** a cruiser; **d** a ferry boat; **e** a liner; **f** a punt; **g** a rowing boat; **h** a submarine; **i** a tanker; **j** a yacht.

2 Which of them would have funnels, guns, masts, oars, passengers?

3 Where on a ship would you find: **a** the bow; **b** the bridge; **c** the keel; **d** the rudder; **e** the stern?

4 What would you call left- and right-hand sides of a ship or boat?

Rescue in the Pacific

THE rescue in the Southern Ocean by Richard Broadhead, 29, the British solo yachtsman, of Jacques de Roux, a fellow competitor, was one of the most remarkable in the history of sailing, Robin Knox-Johnston said yesterday.

5 Mr Knox-Johnston, organising chairman of the single-handed round-the-world race in which two yachtsmen were taking part said that 'it was an amazing operation.'

10 The rescue operation took 59 hours to complete by Friday. The yachts were part of a fleet of 17 which began the 27,000-mile voyage on August 28. Only 10 are

15 still competing.

The rescue took place at 55 degrees South, 124 degrees West, about 1,800 miles from land and far from the major shipping lanes.

20 It was made possible by a French-made Argos satellite tracking **transponder** fitted on the race yachts.

A special distress signal was

25 transmitted by the Argos device when M. de Roux, 43, commander of the French Navy's submarine navigation school, was rolled through **360 degrees** by

30 hurricane-force winds which

dismasted *Skoiern III*, his 43ft cutter.

The race headquarters are in **Newport**, Rhode Island, the

35 starting and finishing point of the four-stage voyage, which has compulsory staging points at Cape Town, Sydney and Rio de Janeiro. It took them 12 hours to alert the

40 British yachtsman of the plight of *Skoiern III*.

An aluminium yacht, *Skoiern III* was close to sinking when the British yacht finally went

45 alongside to rescue its skipper on Friday night.

Because it takes two hours for a computer which analyses the information from the satellites to

50 produce its findings, the last two hours of the rescue were a masterpiece of long-range **dead reckoning** by a special navigation team in Newport.

55 Contact with Mr Broadhead was via an international network

Newport: in the USA

transponder: an electronic system for communication

dead-reckoning: navigating without benefit of observation of the sun

360 degrees: in a circle, returning right way up after being underwater

of radio 'hams', the key link being 'Matthew', a New Zealand radio operator who spoke to the British **60** yachtsman midway between Sydney and Cape Horn.

They directed Mr Broadhead with his 52ft. *Perseverance of Medina*, to the south of the **65** Frenchman, then back up the previous known track of *Skoiern III*.

From *Yacht Rescue Amazing, says Knox-Johnston* by Tony Fairchild in the *Daily Telegraph*

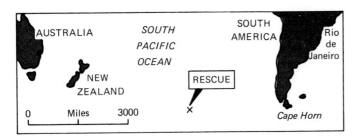

Exercise 1

Some multiple-choice questions depend on reading details carefully. We can always check, for example, the names of the yachtsmen here or their ages, but some details must be worked out.

*Choose the correct answer, a, b or c; only **one** answer is correct in each case.*

1 The rescue operation began on
   a Tuesday.
   b Wednesday.
   c Thursday.
   (How many hours in a day? When did it finish?)

2 How many yachts had dropped out of the race before *Skoiern III*?
   a Six.
   b Seven.
   c Ten.
   (Before!)

3 The distress signal was first transmitted to
   a Newport.
   b New Zealand.
   c the British yacht.
   (First!)

4 At the time of the rescue, the ships were on the _____ stage of their voyage.
   a second
   b third
   c last
   (Which way were they going?)

5 Mr Broadhead was finally contacted by
   a satellite.
   b radio from Newport.
   c radio from New Zealand.

Exercise 2

Find words or phrases in the passage that are similar in meaning to the following. The number in brackets indicates the paragraph where the word or phrase is to be found.

1 participating (2)
2 a number of ships (3)
3 journey by sea (3)
4 very strong wind (5)
5 warn (6)
6 from a great distance (8)
7 amateurs (9)
8 vital connection (9)
9 halfway (9)

Exercise 3

● A course, journey, route, travel (*v. and n.*), voyage

Choose the correct word to complete the following. Use plural forms where appropriate.

In the ¹_____ of his ²_____ round the world Richard Broadhead took part in an amazing rescue. It took place in the South Pacific, a long way from the normal ³_____ between America and Australia. Broadhead heard that another yachtsman was in trouble and changed ⁴_____ to save him. The message had ⁵_____ from the race headquarters in the USA on a ⁶_____ of thousands of miles by a complicated ⁷_____, a series of amateur radio operators. Men like Mr Broadhead may be fond of ⁸_____, but they see little on their ⁹_____ except the sea. It is a very different form of ¹⁰_____ from the ¹¹_____s we make every weekend by car.

● B advice, notice, sign, signal, warning

Choose the correct word to complete the following.

1 SOS, SOS, SOS transmitted by a radio is a
   _____.
2 DANGER! KEEP CLEAR. (This is a _____ that contains a _____.)
3 % is a _____ that means percentage.
4 One Way Street is a traffic _____, but a red light is a _____ of danger or an order to stop on the road or railway.
5 'I should give up smoking if I were you,' is _____ that you might give to a friend. 'If you don't, you will be seriously ill' is a

● C drop, fall, sink, slip, spill

*Use each verb, **at least once**, in the correct form to complete the following.*

1 We had bad luck in the restaurant last night. The waiter _____ on the polished floor, _____ down, and as he did so, _____ the tray he was carrying and _____ the soup all over my new suit.
2 She _____ the coin into the fountain and watched it _____ to the bottom.
3 Rain has been _____ steadily all day and the barometer is still _____, too.
4 The boy _____ on the wet stones and _____ into the water. A woman _____ the shopping bag she was carrying and jumped in to save him.
5 They _____ depth charges into the water, trying to hit the submarine that had _____ the merchant ship with a torpedo.

Crime

Introductory exercise

Before looking at the passage below, answer these questions.

1   If someone commits a crime, he/she may be:
    a convicted; *b* tried; *c* accused; *d* charged;
    e sent to prison; *f* arrested. Put these actions
    in the correct order of normal events.

2   When a trial takes place in court for a serious
    offence, what part is played by: *a* the
    defendant; *b* the defending counsel; *c* the
    judge; *d* the jury; *e* the prosecuting counsel;
    f the witnesses?

Chief Justice of the United States

Republicans and Democrats:
members or supporters of the two
main political parties in the USA
District Attorney: state prosecutor
in the USA
majority opinion: The Supreme
Court's decisions are the result of
a vote.
railroad: railway in British English

Earl Warren was appointed as Chief Justice of the United States
when he was 62, by President Eisenhower, who saw in him (as
we all did) a dependable, conservative **Republican**, an old
District Attorney very much for God and mother and very
5 much against sin, crime, national health insurance, the
Communists and the **Democrats.** Eisenhower came to say that
the appointment of Warren was 'The biggest damn-fool mistake
I ever made.'
    Within eight months of Warren's appointment the Court was
10 faced with the historic case of the little black girl who had to
walk two miles to a segregated school (the case of Brown v. the
Board of Education of Topeka, Kansas). And the Court ordered
the integrating of whites and blacks in American public schools,
and so set off the charge for the black revolution of our day. The
15 **majority opinion** was written by Earl Warren. He went on to
champion the rights of accused criminals to have free legal aid,
and even the right of convicted criminals to be released if they
were not told, at the moment of arrest, of this new privilege. He
helped to reshape the old election districts of the country that
20 had manifestly ignored dramatic shifts in population.
    What produced this profound shift of sympathy, this chemical
change in his character? We are on the dangerous ground of
amateur psychiatry. But I hazard a guess. When he was about
twelve or thirteen, there was a workers' strike on the Southern
25 Pacific **railroad.** His father was one of its ringleaders. The men
stayed out for the best part of a year. Warren recalled in private
many years later: 'We had a hard time of it in our home getting
enough food to eat.'

This trauma must have faded, as such things will in healthy
30 boys. But not long after his appointment to the Court, I imagine,
he must have sometimes thought about the time when he was one
of the people, the hungry people, in opposition. Anyway, some
subdued element of his character rose to the surface and
transformed him. And he became, according to taste, either the
35 heroic judge of our time or 'the biggest damn-fool mistake'
Eisenhower ever made.

From *The Americans* by Alistair Cooke (abridged)

Exercise 1

*Choose the most likely meaning of these words
or phrases in the context of the passage.*
1 **appointed** (line 1): *a* chosen *b* elected (Was
   there a vote on it?)
2 **historic** (line 10): *a* now famous *b* taking
   place in history (Look up **historical** in the
   dictionary.)
3 **segregated** (line 11): *a* private and distant
   b separated on racial grounds (So what
   does **integrating** mean in this context?)
4 **set off the charge** (line 14): *a* led forces into
   battle *b* lit the fuse that later caused an
   explosion
5 **champion** (line 16): *a* the best in the world
   b speak in support of
6 **manifestly** (line 20): *a* openly *b* secretly
   (What is a **manifesto**?)
7 **sympathy** (line 21): *a* attraction
   b understanding feeling
8 **hazard** (line 23): *a* luck *b* risk (Grammar!)
9 **ringleader** (line 25): central figure in a fight
   a for authority *b* against authority
10 **recalled** (line 26): *a* remembered *b* reminded
   (Structure!)

Exercise 2

*Choose the correct answer, a, b, or c. Only **one**
answer is correct in each case.*
1 Eisenhower chose Warren as Chief Justice
   because he
   a loved God and his mother.
   b was a conservative Republican.
   c was an old District Attorney.
2 Which of the following should be a
   qualification for a judge — a dislike of
   a crime?
   b national health insurance?
   c sin?
3 Eisenhower regretted the appointment
   because Warren
   a betrayed him.
   b made unexpected decisions.
   c was inefficient.
4 Warren wanted to change the law so that
   convicted criminals would be released if they
   a had not been advised of their rights when
      arrested.
   b had not been given free legal aid.
   c were proved innocent.
5 He helped to change election districts
   because they were
   a ignorant.
   b illegal.
   c unequal.
6 The writer guesses that Warren changed after
   becoming Chief Justice because he was
   reminded of
   a his years of political opposition.
   b his youth as a strike leader.
   c hunger in childhood.

Exercise 3

Find words or phrases in the passage that are similar in meaning to the following. The number in brackets indicates the paragraph where the word or phrase is to be found.

1 reliable (1)
2 confronted (2)
3 help (2)
4 set free (2)
5 areas (2)
6 deep (3)
7 were on strike (3)
8 completely changed (4)

Exercise 4

● **A accuse, arrest, charge, inform, warn, threaten**

Use each verb, **once only**, in the correct form to complete the following.

When a police officer ¹_____ someone for a crime, it is not enough for him to ²_____ him of it, saying: 'You did it, didn't you?' He must formally ³_____ the person with the crime and ⁴_____ him that anything he says may be used in evidence against him. He must also ⁵_____ him of his legal rights, but must not use force or ⁶_____ him with it to obtain a confession.

● **B in fact, in particular, in private, in public, in secret**

Choose the correct phrase to complete the following.

Warren confessed ¹_____, presumably when the author was present, that he had been hungry when his father was on strike, although of course he did not make this statement ²_____. People were surprised by the change in Warren, and Republicans ³_____ were angry about it. No doubt, if he had still been Chief Justice, he would have disapproved of President Nixon's habit of recording his conversations with people ⁴_____, without their knowledge, but ⁵_____ Warren retired when Nixon was elected.

● **C fade, fail, faint, lighten, weaken**

Use each verb, **at least once**, in the Past tense to complete the following.

1 The colour _____ from the dress after she washed it.
2 His obvious prejudices _____ his claim to be a fair judge.
3 She _____ when she heard the news of her son's conviction.
4 His appeal against the conviction _____.
5 The sky _____ after the storm.
6 In time, the bitter memories of his childhood _____.

Meeting the rich

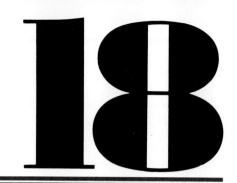

Introductory exercise

Before looking at the passage below, study the following family tree and answer the questions on it.

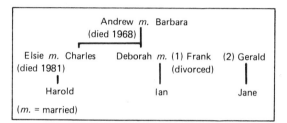

```
                 Andrew  m.  Barbara
                 (died 1968)

Elsie  m.  Charles    Deborah  m. (1) Frank    (2) Gerald
(died 1981)                       (divorced)

     Harold              Ian                   Jane

(m. = married)
```

1 What relation is Harold to Charles, Barbara, Deborah, Ian?
2 What relation is Barbara to Charles, Harold, Gerald?
3 What relation is Deborah to Barbara, Charles, Harold, Gerald, Frank?
4 What relation is Gerald to Charles, Ian?
5 Which of the characters is a widow, widower, stepson?
6 Which of them was a grandfather, daughter-in-law, sister-in-law?

Father

I sipped the drink. The old man licked his lips watching me.

'Tell me about yourself, Mr Marlowe. I suppose I have a right to ask?'

'**Sure**, but there's very little to tell. I'm thirty-three years old, went to **college** once and can still speak English if there's any demand for it. There
5 isn't much in my trade. I worked for Mr Wilde, the District Attorney, as an investigator once. His chief investigator, a man named Bernie Ohls, called me and told me you wanted to see me. I'm unmarried because I don't like policemen's wives.'

'And a little bit of a cynic,' the old man smiled. 'You didn't like working
10 for Wilde?'

'I was **fired.** For insubordination. I **test very high** on insubordination, General.'

'I always did myself, sir. I'm glad to hear it. What do you know about my family?'
15 'I'm told you are a widower and have two young daughters, both pretty and both wild. One of them has been married three times, the last time to an ex-**bootlegger**, who went in the trade by the name of Rusty Regan. That's all I heard, General.'

'Did any of it strike you as peculiar?'
20 'The Rusty Regan part, maybe. But I always got along with bootleggers myself.'

He smiled his faint economical smile. 'It seems I do too. I'm very fond of Rusty.'

From *The Big Sleep* by Raymond Chandler

Sure: Certainly (UK)
college: university (UK)
fired: sacked (UK)
test very high: score very high marks (UK)
bootlegger: person selling alcohol illegally (during the period of Prohibition in the USA — 1919–33)

Exercise 1

Choose the most likely meaning of these words in the context of the passage.

1 **sipped** (line 1): drank *a* slowly, just a little *b* all at once
2 **licked** (line 1): a gesture, using *a* the hands *b* the tongue (In fact, the General was forbidden to drink anything alcoholic by his doctors.)
3 **insubordination** (line 11): *a* incompetence *b* disobedience
4 **wild** (line 16): *a* savage *b* uncontrolled (Daughters.)
5 **economical** (line 22): *a* having to do with economics *b* using the minimum effort (Look up **economic** in the dictionary.)

Exercise 2

Passages like this contain a great deal that is *fact* and more that may be *inferred*. Multiple-choice questions may expect you to understand the facts, but also to form an overall impression of what is going on.

● A

Fact: If you were the General you could fill in a form about Marlowe from the conversation here.

Write what you would have discovered.

```
Name: _____

Age: _____

Marital Status: _____

Education: _____

Previous Experience: _____

_____

Reason for leaving previous job: _____

_____
```

● B

For the other characters mentioned, we have less information and in most cases can only make guesses.

*Complete the form, **as far as possible**, for General Sternwood, Mrs Regan, Carmen Sternwood, Rusty Regan.*

● C

*Choose the correct answer, a, b or c. Only **one** answer is correct in each case.*

1 Marlowe
  a no longer has any contact with the District Attorney's office.
  b was once a policeman.
  c lost his job because he was too cynical.
2 Marlowe
  a has asked a lot of questions about the General's family.
  b knew Rusty Regan when he was a bootlegger.
  c doesn't know very much about the family.
3 The General
  a disapproved of his daughter's last marriage.
  b thought it was peculiar.
  c likes her husband.

● D

Inference: This depends in part on understanding Marlowe's way of talking,

e.g. Does he really mean that he doesn't usually speak English? Or does he mean that he has a personal definition of what speaking English means?
Does he think that he could only marry a policeman's wife? Or does he mean that he doesn't think policemen should get married (because of their job)?

You will not be asked to explain things like this, but an understanding helps to answer questions on the relationship between Marlowe and the General.

Find evidence to suggest that Marlowe is independent in his attitudes, but also tolerant, and that the General respects him for it.

*Choose the correct answer, a, b or c. Only **one** answer is correct in each case.*

1 Marlowe
   a objects to the General's questions.
   b talks to him naturally.
   c thinks he is a strict father.

2 The General
   a likes Marlowe's openness.
   b demands to know all about him before employing him.
   c thinks he is too independent.

Daughter

Mrs Regan had a drink. She took a swallow from it and gave me a cool level stare over the rim of the glass.

'So you're a private detective,' she said. 'I didn't know they really existed, except in books. Or else they were greasy little men snooping around hotels.'

There was nothing in that for me, so I let it drift with the current. She put her glass down on the flat arm of the chaise-longue and flashed an emerald and touched her hair. She said slowly: 'How did you like Dad?'

'I liked him,' I said.

'He liked Rusty. I suppose you know who Rusty is?'

'Uh- huh.'

'Rusty was earthy and vulgar at times, but he was very real. And he was a lot of fun for Dad. Rusty shouldn't have gone off like that. Dad feels very badly about it, although he won't say so. Or did he?'

'He said something about it.'

'You're not much of a gusher, are you, Mr Marlowe? But he wants to find him, doesn't he?'

I stared at her politely through a pause. 'Yes and no,' I said.

'That's hardly an answer. Do you think you can find him?'

'I didn't say I was going to try. Why not try the Missing Persons Bureau? They have the organisation. It's not a one-man job.'

'Oh Dad wouldn't hear of the police being brought into it.' She looked at me smoothly across her glass again, emptied it, and rang a bell. A maid came into the room by a side door. She was a middle-aged woman with a long yellow gentle face, a long nose, no chin, large wet eyes. She looked like a nice old horse that has been turned out to pasture after long service. Mrs Regan waved the empty glass at her and she mixed another drink and handed it to her and left the room, without a word, without a glance in my direction. When the door shut Mrs Regan said: 'How will you go about it then?'

'How and when did he skip out?'

'Didn't Dad tell you?'

I grinned at her with my head on one side. She flushed. Her hot black eyes looked **mad**. 'I don't see what there is to be cagey about,' she snapped. 'And I don't like your manners.'

'I'm not **crazy** about yours,' I said. 'I didn't ask to see you.'

mad: angry (UK)
crazy: excited (UK)

From *The Big Sleep* by Raymond Chandler

Exercise 1

Decide on the probable meaning of these words in the context of the passage.

1 **a swallow** (line 1): Is this the same as 'a sip'? (Note **emptied**, line 23.)
2 **the rim** (line 2): What part of the glass? (Over the rim.)
3 **greasy** (line 4): Dirty? Unpleasantly slippery? Or both? (Note **little**, line 4.)
4 **snooping** (line 4): Looking, but imagine the circumstances.
5 **chaise-longue** (line 7): a piece of furniture, but what sort?
6 **emerald** (line 7): something that **flashes**. (She is very rich.)
7 **earthy** (line 12): agricultural, or is she talking about his conversation?
8 **a gusher** (line 16): slang, but why is Mrs Regan irritated by Marlowe?
9 **pasture** (line 26): What happens to horses when they get old?
10 **skip out** (line 31): slang, but what has Rusty done?
11 **flushed** (line 33): She went red, but with embarrassment, or anger? (Look up **blush** in the dictionary.)
12 **cagey** (line 34): slang, but how has Marlowe been answering her questions?
13 **snapped** (line 34): said, obviously, but in what sort of voice?

Exercise 2

This interview takes place soon after Marlowe's meeting with the General, Mrs Regan's father.

● A

Find evidence, by comparing the two passages, of differences between her attitude to Marlowe and her father's. Consider this in terms of respect and politeness (personal, and towards a visitor). Is she interested in him, concerned about her husband? Who is she most concerned about?

● B

Find evidence to suggest that Mrs Regan is used to having her own way. Why does Marlowe annoy her? What makes her angry? How do we know?

● C

*Choose the correct answer, a, b or c. Only **one** answer is correct in each case.*

1 Marlowe _____ Mrs Regan's insult.
   a doesn't understand
   b ignores
   c reacts to
2 He
   a refuses to answer her questions.
   b tells her what she wants to know.
   c keeps her guessing.
3 The police have not been called in because the General
   a doesn't want publicity.
   b doesn't trust their organisation.
   c thinks one man can do the job better.
4 While the second drink was being mixed,
   a Mrs Regan did not look at Marlowe.
   b the maid did not look at Marlowe.
   c Marlowe did not look at the maid.
5 a Mrs Regan trusts Marlowe, but thinks he is rude.
   b Marlowe trusts Mrs Regan, but thinks she is rude.
   c Neither trusts the other, and each thinks the other is rude.

Exercise 3

● **A** **prove, test, try** (*two meanings*)**, try on, try out**

*Use each verb, **at least once,** in the correct form to complete the following.*

1 At the beginning, Mrs Regan ¹_____ Marlowe to see if he would react to her manner. Then she ²_____ to make him tell her about his conversation with her father. She thought he knew more than he said, but she could not ³_____ it. Marlowe did not admit that he was ⁴_____ to find Rusty. He suggested that the family should ⁵_____ contacting the Missing Persons Bureau instead.
2 When shopping for clothes we usually _____ them _____ before we buy them.
3 We go out in a car before buying it to see if we like it — this is called _____ it _____. (Notice the difference in structure with the different meaning of **try**.)

● **B** **gaze, glance, glimpse, stare** (*all n. and v.*)

gaze = look at for a long time with pleasure
glance = look at for a moment
glimpse = see for a moment
stare = look at for a long time rudely

Choose the best word, in either noun or verb form, to complete the following.

1 I love to _____ at the stars on a clear night.
2 I caught a _____ of her as she hurried past the window.
3 She went out without a _____ in my direction.
4 Mrs Regan _____ at Marlowe to prove her superiority.

(Note that when Marlowe 'stared at her politely', he was only pretending to be polite!)

Lexical Progress Test 3

You must choose the word or phrase which best completes each sentence. For each question, 1 to 25, indicate the correct answer, A, B, C or D. The time for the test is 20 minutes.

1 I'm glad to hear he's _____ completely after his illness.
A got over B healed C recovered D repaired

2 Are you sure those shoes _____ you? They're not too tight, then.
A fit B go with C match D suit

3 The main purpose in keeping fit is to feel more pleasure in being _____.
A alive B conscious C live D lively

4 He broke his leg in a car _____.
A blow B crash C hit D shock

5 It's time you went out and _____ your own living.
A afforded B earned C gained D won

6 The dress isn't really tight. It'll _____ when you've worn it.
A bend B expand C squeeze D stretch

7 The boat turned over and sank to the _____.
A base B basis C bottom D ground

8 When you've washed up, _____ the plates before you put them away.
A clean B dust C sweep D wipe

9 It's very kind of you to _____ to speak at the meeting.
A accept B agree C approve D consider

10 I've found a marvellous _____ for curried chicken.
A course B prescription C receipt D recipe

11 The elephant fell into a _____ the hunters had set.
A track B trap C trick D trunk

12 The Captain was glad to see land after his long _____.
A excursion B route C travel D voyage

13 You must take _____ of the opportunity you've been given.
A advantage B benefit C occasion D profit

14 See if you can take the bucket through the kitchen without _____ any of the water in it.
A dropping B falling C sinking D spilling

15 The police _____ him of robbing a bank.
A accused B arrested C charged D punished

16 These curtains have _____ since you washed them.
A faded B failed C fainted D lightened

17 Do you mind if I _____ this dress to see if it suits me?
A prove B test C try on D wear out

18 I caught a _____ of her as she walked past the window.
A glance B glimpse C look D sight

19 She was so keen to see her present that she _____ the paper off the parcel.
A broke B smashed C tore D unwrapped

20 The lecture was so _____ that everyone fell asleep.
A bored B dull C exhausted D tired

21 I'm very pleased with my new secretary. Her work is of a high _____.
A condition B degree C capacity D standard

22 Do you think you'll be _____ to play in the match tomorrow?
A fit B healthy C suitable D well

23 They fell in love at first _____.
A glimpse B look C sight D view

24 I blame all of you, but Stephen in _____.
A his own B particular C private D special

25 There's a big _____ outside his house, advertising it for sale.
A advice B message C notice D signal

72

Sport

19

Introductory exercise

Before looking at the passage below, answer these questions.

1   In which games or sports would you be likely to use: **a** a bat; **b** a club; **c** a racket; **d** a rod; **e** a stick? What would they be made of?

2   Which games are played with: **a** an oval ball; **b** a red ball stitched together; **c** a small black ball; **d** a small white ball; **e** a round, flat rubber disc (puck)?

The most dramatic Cup Final

Wembley

The Cup Final is still the only football match guaranteed to attract 100,000 spectators to Wembley Stadium every year, even though it is also shown on television by law. It is a great public event, as much as a game of football, and 30 years ago, when England played fewer
5   internationals and the European Cup had not been invented, it seemed even more so. I was very excited when my father managed to get two tickets for the Final in 1953, though I did not realise then that it would be the most memorable ever played.

The teams, Blackpool and Bolton Wanderers, both came from the
10 north, but almost everyone in England wanted Blackpool to win because the greatest player of his generation, Stanley Matthews, then 40 years old, was playing for them in what would surely be his last Cup Final. He had twice reached the Final before, but each time a cup winner's medal had eluded him..

15 The atmosphere before the match was traditional, but electric. The crowd sang songs for an hour, led by a conductor in the middle of the pitch. At one end there was a sea of orange, with Blackpool supporters roaring for their team; at the other, there were black and white scarves, hats and banners waving in the air for Bolton.

20 The game began on a false note for Blackpool. Farm, their goalkeeper, had an attack of nerves, and let a simple shot bounce over his outstretched arm in the first minute. Twenty minutes later, he made another terrible mistake to give Bolton their second goal. It looked as if Matthews would be disappointed once again. But then
25 one of the Bolton half-backs, Bell, was injured, and in those days no substitutes were allowed. He limped along the wing on one leg, and Blackpool, inspired by Matthews and the tireless Mortensen at centre forward, began to recover, and Mortensen scored.

Early in the second half, however, disaster struck again. The injured
30 Bell bravely headed a goal for Bolton, and though Mortensen again reduced the arrears, Bolton were still holding on to their 3–2 lead with four minutes to go.

I can still remember Mortensen placing the ball for a free kick over 30 metres from the Bolton goal, just in front of where I was sitting, as
35 if it were yesterday. He swung his boot. No one moved, not even Hanson in the Bolton goal. Then the whole terrace in orange colours to my left went mad with joy. The ball had travelled so fast that we could hardly believe it had hit the back of the net. Two minutes later, the old master, Matthews, made one of his inimitable runs down the
40 right wing, and centred for Perry to score the winning goal.

A few years later I met a Blackpool supporter who knew some of their players, and he reminded me that Taylor, the inside-right, had gone over to speak to Mortensen as he was placing the ball for the free kick. Apparently the conversation went like this:
45 Taylor: 'What are you going to do, Stan?'
Mortensen: 'Shoot.'
Taylor: (in disgust) 'You must be daft.' ('Daft' means 'crazy' in the north of England.)

Exercise 1

Decide on the probable meaning of these words or phrases in the context of the passage.
1 **eluded** (line 14): *a* beaten *b* got away from
2 **electric** (line 15): has to do with *a* lightning *b* excitement
3 **limped** (line 26): on one leg!
4 **tireless** (line 27): *a* incapable of getting tired *b* tired and weary
5 **reduced the arrears** (line 31): What was the score now? Who were still winning?

Exercise 2

The questions here all relate to your overall impression of the passage.

Choose the answer that best seems to summarise a paragraph or a number of sentences.

1 The Cup Final
   a has long been considered a national spectacle.
   b used to be an important event.
   c in 1953 was expected to be the greatest ever played.
2 Before the match
   a most people thought Blackpool was the better team.
   b people favoured Blackpool for sentimental reasons.
   c support for the two teams was evenly divided.
3 The supporters of the two clubs were
   a aggressive towards each other.
   b mixed up among the crowd.
   c mostly separated.
4 In the first half, Bolton
   a had all the luck.
   b played much better than Blackpool.
   c took advantage of Blackpool's errors.
5 When Mortensen scored the third goal
   a it seemed inevitable.
   b Blackpool were ahead at last.
   c he was following his instinct.

Exercise 3

● A depressing/depressed, disappointing/ disappointed, disgusting/disgusted, disillusioned

Read the following comments and answer the questions about them, using one of the words above in your answer.

1 'I was looking forward to going to India for a holiday, but now I've had to cancel it.'
How does the speaker feel? How would you describe what has happened?

2 'People who stub out their cigarettes in cups, especially when there is liquid in them, make me feel sick.'
How does the speaker feel? How would you describe their behaviour?

3 'Sally's broken off her engagement to me, and I don't seem to have any energy.'
How does the speaker feel?

4 'You can't rely on women. She said she loved me, and now she's going out with her boss.'
How does the speaker feel?

5 'It's no good turning on the television. The news is all wars and strikes, and the plays are full of unhappy couples.'
What does the speaker think about the programmes?

● B game(s), match(es), sport(s)

Choose the correct word to complete the following. Use plural forms where appropriate.

1 In Britain, outdoor ¹_____ has always been encouraged as part of education at the public schools, but when I was at school this meant compulsory team ²_____ like cricket and rugby, with occasional ³_____ against other schools. The only ⁴_____ permitted were boxing, fencing and athletics, and there was a school ⁵_____ day, when the athletics finals were held. Now a more liberal attitude allows individual ⁶_____ like chess and golf, and ⁷_____ like skiing in winter.

2 He won a gold medal at the Olympic _____.

3 _____, set and _____ to Miss Navratilova, the new Wimbledon champion!

4 Many people think boxing is not a _____ at all, and boxing _____ should be banned. Some schools have replaced it with karate.

● C rock, shake, wave

Choose the correct verb to complete the following expressions.

1 _____ hands
2 _____ your head
3 _____ a flag
4 _____ the baby to sleep
5 _____ goodbye to someone
6 Don't _____ the boat.

Travel

20

Introductory exercise

Before looking at the passage below, answer these questions.

1 What sort of work do the following do on the railway? **a** a booking clerk; **b** an engine driver; **c** a fireman; **d** a guard; **e** a porter; **f** a stationmaster?

2 If you were travelling with a few friends on a train, would you try to book a carriage, a compartment or a wagon?

3 What would you do if you wanted to warn the engine driver of an emergency?

Overcoming Indian bureaucracy

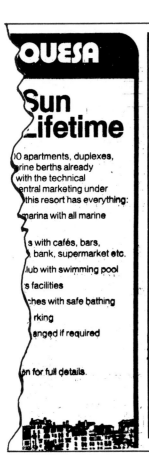

OUESA

Sun Lifetime

)0 apartments, duplexes,
rine berths already
with the technical
entral marketing under
this resort has everything:

marina with all marine

s with cafés, bars,
bank, supermarket etc.

lub with swimming pool

s facilities

ches with safe bathing

rking

anged if required

on for full details.

Bureaucracy is one of the great Indian hate words. It bears down upon the Indian much more than the traveller and one should,
5 therefore, not go on about it to Indians, who must suffer it constantly. The traveller will meet the bureaucracy principally at railway stations while trying to
10 purchase a ticket, when he will be asked to fill in forms and stand in a number of queues. It is best to set aside a whole morning for this exercise. Again, be patient. If the
15 ticket clerk asks you to write a letter to the head ticket clerk – a whole desk away – explaining *why* you want to change your journey date, do not explode into phrases such as
20 'my bloody business' or 'this bloody country'. Sit down and write the letter, including as much useless detail as possible. For example:

To the Chief Reservations
25   Officer
Eastern Railway
Howrah Station, Calcutta

Dear Sir,
  Yesterday I purchased two first-
30 class single tickets, Howrah to McCluskieganj (Bihar state), together with first-class sleeping reservations on the Doon Express, train number nine down, leaving
35 Howrah at 21.05 on February 3. I now find that, due to a family bereavement, I should like to travel by the same train on February 5.
  Trusting you can expedite
40 matters and oblige. I am, yours sincerely_____. My passport number is _____.
My age is _____.
Fold this letter and present it to the
45 head clerk. He will do his best for you. That is how things work in India.
  It sounds depressing. But the rewards of coming to terms with it
50 are great. The Indian Subcontinent is a most wonderful and fascinating place, filled with great beauty and antiquity, where it is still possible to experience the sensations of the
55 traveller rather than the tourist.

con-men: people who get money by deceit

Ruins lack signposted explanations; views are without car parks and mounted telescopes. The traveller must reach them using his 60 own resources and energy and, by doing so, he will be helped and befriended by almost every Indian he meets. For Indians, the minorities of beggars, **con-men** and 65 bureaucrats apart, are usually generous with their time and curiosity.

From *How to Beat the Beggary* by Ian Jack in the *Sunday Times Magazine* (abridged)

Exercise 1

Choose the most likely meaning of these words or phrases in the context of the passage.

1 **bears down upon** (lines 2–3): *a* disgusts *b* depresses
2 **go on about** (line 5): *a* continue complaining about *b* travel around
3 **set aside** (lines 12–13): *a* be prepared to spend...(on) *b* put on one side
4 **bereavement** (line 37): *a* quarrel *b* loss, because of death
5 **rewards** (line 49): has to do with *a* money *b* pleasure
6 **coming to terms with** (line 49): *a* agreeing about *b* reaching an acceptance of

Exercise 2

*Decide which of the following statements best expresses the real meaning of the passage. Choose **one** statement, a, b or c, in each case.*

1 In conversation with Indians about bureaucracy, one should
   a draw their attention to it to improve matters.
   b never mention it to avoid offending them.
   c realise that they are more aware of it than foreigners.
2 The best way to deal with bureaucracy in Indian railway stations is to
   a accept the customs of the country.
   b adopt an independent attitude.
   c fill in forms and write letters.

3 The value of conforming to Indian customs is that the traveller will
   a be given special treatment.
   b be able to appreciate the country better.
   c find them fascinating.
4 Visiting historical monuments in India, the traveller will
   a be angry because nothing is explained.
   b enjoy them more because he has discovered them for himself.
   c have the advantages he is used to in Europe.
5 The majority of Indians
   a behave like bureaucrats towards travellers.
   b go out of their way to help them.
   c are unwilling to give them much information.

Exercise 3

Find words or phrases in the passage that are similar in meaning to the following. The number in brackets indicates the paragraph where the word or phrase is to be found.

1 mainly (1)
2 buy (1)
3 complete (1)
4 lose your temper and use (1)
5 arrange (2)
6 have not got (3)

Exercise 4

● **bend, curve, fold, wrap**

Choose the correct verb to describe the following actions.

1 What do you do when you put a letter in a small envelope?
2 What do you do when you make a parcel to contain a present?
3 What do you do when you drop something and have to pick it up?

4 You couldn't fold an iron bar, even if you were very strong, but you might be able to _____ it into a curve.
5 Roads can either _____ or _____, but, if you climb a tree and go out onto a branch, it will _____ under your weight.

How *not* to go to France

IF YOU ARE THINKING about going abroad and want to preserve your ardour for travelling, don't pore over a little book called "Collins' Pocket Interpreters: France," which I picked up in London. Each page has a list of English expressions, one under the other, which
5 gives them the form of verse. The French translations are run alongside. The volume contains three times as many expressions to use when one is in trouble as when everything is going all right. This, my own experience has shown, is about the right ratio, but God spare me from some of the difficulties for which the traveller
10 is prepared in Mr. Collins' melancholy narrative poem. I am going to leave out the French translations because, for one thing, people who get involved in the messes and tangles we are coming to invariably forget their French and scream in English, anyway.

Trouble really starts in the canto called "In the Customs Shed."
15 Here we have: "I cannot open my case." "I have lost my keys." "Help me to close this case." "I did not know that I had to pay." "I don't want to pay so much." "I cannot find my porter." "Have you seen porter 153?" That last query is a little master stroke of writing, I think, for in those few words we have a graphic picture of
20 a tourist lost in a jumble of thousands of bags and scores of customs men, looking frantically for one of at least a hundred and fifty-three porters. We feel that the tourist will not find porter 153, and the note of frustration has been struck.

Our tourist (accompanied by his wife, I like to think) finally gets
25 on the train for Paris having lost his keys and not having found his porter — and it comes time presently to go to the dining car, although he probably has no appetite, for the customs men, of course, have had to break open that one suitcase. Now, I think, it is the wife who begins to crumble: "Someone has taken my seat."
30 "Excuse me, sir, that seat is mine." "I cannot find my ticket!" "I have left my ticket in the compartment." "I will go and look for it." "I have left my gloves (my purse) in the dining car." Here the note of frenzied disintegration, so familiar to all travellers abroad, is sounded. Next comes "The Sleeper," which begins, ominously,

35 with "What is the matter?" and ends with "May I open the window?" "Can you open this window, please?" We realize, of course, that *nobody* is going to be able to open the window and that the tourist and his wife will suffocate. In this condition they arrive in Paris, and the scene there, on the crowded station **40** platform, is done with superb economy of line: "I have left something in the train." "A parcel, an overcoat." "A mackintosh, a stick." "An umbrella, a camera." "A fur, a suitcase." The travellers have now begun to go completely to pieces.

From *Alarms and Diversions* by James Thurber (abridged)

Exercise 1

Choose the most likely meaning of these words in the context of the passage.
1 **pore over** (line 2): *a* glance at *b* study carefully
2 **picked up** (line 3): *a* took from the ground *b* bought in a shop
3 **tangles** (line 12): *a* confusing situations *b* terrifying situations
4 **graphic** (line 19): *a* drawn on the page *b* easy to imagine
5 **jumble** (line 20): *a* disordered mass *b* neat pile
6 **scores** (line 20): *a* hundreds *b* lots (How many in a score?)
7 **crumble** (line 29): *a* lose control *b* break bread into pieces

Exercise 2

Appreciation of humour like this depends on accepting the writer's idea of deliberately creating an absurd situation and then exploiting it.

Study the passage and answer the following questions.
1 Why is the book depressing to read, and what has the writer done to make it sound more depressing?
2 Why does he suggest that it is written in verse? Which other expressions emphasise this? (There are two.)

3 Having convinced us that the book tells a story, how does he make an innocent phrase sound ridiculous by drawing attention to it in Paragraph 3?
4 Why does the series of expressions at the end suggest the travellers are going mad? What is their real purpose?

Exercise 3

Find words or phrases in the passage that are similar in meaning to the following. The number in brackets indicates the paragraph where the word or phrase is to be found.
1 enthusiasm (1)
2 book (1)
3 omit (1)
4 always (1)
5 inquiry (2)
6 wildly excited (3)
7 in a manner warning of disaster (3)
8 choke (3)

Exercise 4

● **accustomed, common, familiar, ordinary, rude**

Choose the correct word to complete the following.

1 They get on very well because they have _____ interests (or: interests in _____).
2 He was a _____ figure on the train; I always saw him sitting in the corner in his _____ seat.
3 Are you _____ with (or: _____ to) this sort of work?
4 It was a rather _____ day. Nothing special happened.
5 He's very _____. He has no idea of good manners.
6 Earthquakes are quite _____ in his country. They happen every week.

NOTE: A member of your family is a **relation**, or **relative**.

Employment

Introductory exercise

Before looking at the passage below, answer these questions.

1 Can you complete these pairs, which are usually thought of as opposites?

   e.g. having a job and being **out of work**

   a i_____ and expenditure; **b** profit and l_____; **c** employment and u_____; **d** employer and e_____.

2 In what circumstances could you claim: **a** an allowance; **b** expenses; **c** a pension; **d** a redundancy payment; **e** unemployment benefit?

Earlier retirement?

IF YOU ask the man in the street, whether the street be in **Manchester** or **Mannheim** how we should tackle the unemployment problem, the chances are that somewhere in his reply he will mention early retirement.

It is not difficult to see why. Ten years ago this objective was being pursued on social grounds, and there is a popular sense of justice in the old yielding to the young, the employed to the unemployed.

But, of course, it is not as easy as that. If you eliminate one job, you do not automatically create another. Indeed, broadly speaking, you will be lucky to create half a job and more likely one-third at a time of rising productivity and stagnant demand. And even some of the jobs you create, perhaps a third of them, will be taken by the non-registered unemployed, further reducing the political appeal of the action.

Then there is the cost. **Actuarially** calculated, German social security contributions will need to double in the next 50 years to meet existing commitments on old age pensions. And with non-wage labour costs over 40 per cent of **payroll,** German employers are already screaming that they can afford no more.

In Belgium and the Netherlands, the sticky moment has already come when benefits have had to be cut to make ends meet. In France, Unedic, the joint employer-union-Government **dole** fund has just collapsed.

In Britain, the Commons Social Services Committee has just made a modest proposal to phase in a unified retirement age of 63, having been warned off more radical ideas by official estimates that existing pension commitments will cost double the present level by the year 2031 and that to cut the retirement age to 60 would cost an immediate £2.5bn. Pensions and associated benefits already consume 17 per cent of Britain's public expenditure.

Men aged 60–64 in the workforce

	1970 %	1979 %	Downward Trend %
Belgium	63.8	33	48
Germany	74.7	39	48
France	65.2	38	42
Britain	86.6	75	13
Netherlands	73.9	59	20
Austria	47.7	26	45
Sweden	79.5	69	13
USA	75.0	61	19

Source: International Institute of Management, Berlin

Manchester, Mannheim: typical industrial cities in Britain and West Germany

actuarially: An actuary is an expert in calculating the rates of insurance.

payroll: the bill for wages

dole: unemployment benefit

From *Unemployment in Europe: III, Why shorter hours are here to stay* by Ian Hargreaves in the *Financial Times* (abridged)

Exercise 1

Choose the most likely meaning of these words or phrases in the context of the passage.

1 **the man in the street** (lines 1–2): *a* the average man *b* someone working on the roads
2 **productivity** (line 22): *a* production of manufactured goods *b* production per person employed
3 **stagnant** (line 22): *a* falling *b* not moving
4 **non-registered** (lines 25–6): refers to *a* people who have never worked since leaving school *b* people who have not put their names down at an employment office
5 **make ends meet** (lines 42–3): refers to *a* economics *b* communication

Exercise 2

These questions test your overall understanding of the passage.

*Choose the correct answer, a, b or c. Only **one** answer is correct in each case.*

1 Most people see early retirement as an answer to unemployment because they think it
   a is more efficient.
   b seems fair.
   c will save money.
2 Establishing an earlier retirement age will not provide the same number of jobs because
   a firms do not need to replace everyone employed at present.
   b governments will be against introducing it because it will be unpopular.
   c most of the jobs will go to people who are not registered at employment offices.
3 German employers are unhappy about the fact that
   a they will have to pay double the contribution towards pensions in future.
   b benefits to people out of work have had to be reduced.
   c the high ratio of social security contributions to wages may be increased.

4 Reducing the retirement age to 60 in Britain would
   a double the expenditure on pensions immediately.
   b use up 17% of Britain's public expenditure.
   c cost a lot more than the present proposal.
5 Judging from the table,
   a the age at retirement is now more or less the same in the countries mentioned.
   b the countries where people used to retire latest have been those most resistant to change.
   c there has been a fall of similar proportions in the percentage of people employed in these age groups.

Exercise 3

Find words or phrases in the passage that are similar in meaning to the following. The number in brackets indicates the paragraph where the word or phrase is to be found.

1 deal with (1)
2 it is likely (1)
3 answer (1)
4 giving way to (2)
5 do away with (3)
6 in general terms (3)
7 complaining bitterly (4)
8 difficult (5)
9 introduce by stages (6)
10 calculations (6)

Exercise 4

● **advantage, benefit, earnings, income, profit, salary, wage(s)**

Choose the correct word to complete the following.

When I was 23, and had just left university and got a job, I went to the Social Security Office. During National Service, I had paid social security stamps out of the miserable ¹_____ I got, but I had put the ²_____ from occasional odd jobs I did at university in my pocket. The kindly clerk at the Office advised me to pay all the social security stamps for my three years at university in order to guarantee full social security ³_____ when I retired. I couldn't see much ⁴_____ in that. He wanted over £100, more than my monthly ⁵_____, and about a quarter of my total annual ⁶_____ after taxes. So I didn't take ⁷_____ of his offer, and when I saved some money and bought some shares on the stock exchange a year later and was lucky enough to make a ⁸_____ of £100, it never occurred to me to give it to the Social Security Office. I'm sure I got a great deal more ⁹_____ out of the holiday I had in Ibiza with the money! 'A bird in the hand is worth two in the bush', says the proverb, and who knows what £100 will be worth in forty years' time?

Paying income tax

 P15 CODING CLAIM

Tax reference [   ]

Please read these notes before you write anything:

Your employer has given you this form because you have not given him form P45. Without a P45 you may pay the wrong tax. If you can get a P45, you need not fill in this form. So
- if you left a job recently, but have not since claimed unemployment benefit, ask your old employer for a P45
- if you have been claiming unemployment benefit, sign off by returning card UB40. A P45 will then be sent to you.

However, you should fill in this form
- if you cannot get a P45, or you have lost it
- if this is your first paid job.

This form will help to give you a correct PAYE code so that you pay the right tax. You may not have to fill in all of it. Please follow the instructions in blue and fill in those sections that apply to you, using BLOCK CAPITALS.

A **Everyone should fill in this section:**

Your surname . . . . Mr/Mrs/Miss/Ms . . . .

Your Christian names or first names . . . .

The name and address of
your new employer . . . .

. . . .

The title or description
of your new job . . . . Your National
Insurance number [ ][ ][ ][ ]

Is this new job your **only** job? If you have a second job, or do part-time or evening work, any payments you receive are part of your income. They are taxable in just the same way as the earnings from your regular job.

Please say YES or NO . . . .

If your answer is 'YES', please turn to page 2. If your answer is 'NO', please fill in section B below.

B Please give details of **any other work** for which you get paid:

The title or description of the job . . . .

The name and address of
the employer . . . .

If you work for
yourself please
write 'self-employed' . . . .

Your works or check number (if any) . . . .

The branch or site
where you work . . . .

The tax reference (if known) . . . .

Your total weekly earnings from
the work before any stoppages £ . . . .

Which is your **main** job? Is it your new job, shown in section A? Or the job shown in section B?

Please write A or B . . . .

If your answer is 'A', please turn to page 2.

If your answer is 'B', please turn straight to page 4: there is no need to fill in pages 2 and 3.

Exercise 1

*Study the form on page 83, then choose the correct answer, a, b, or c, to these questions. Only **one** answer is correct in each case.*

1 What is the form for?
    a To make sure that everyone pays tax.
    b To find out how much tax people should pay.
    c To make sure that employers are paying workers the correct wage rates for the job.

2 *a* Everyone must fill in the form.
    b Everyone must fill in the first section.
    c Some employees must fill in the form.

3 When you fill in the form, you must
    a complete it in capital letters.
    b use a pen with blue ink.
    c complete all of it.

4 After you have filled it in, you must
    a contact your old employer, if you have one.
    b hand it to your new employer.
    c post it to the tax office.

Exercise 2

Read the information about these three new employees of XYZ Co. Imagine you are each of them in turn and answer the questions below.
SARAH FIELD, 16, typist. This is her first job.
JAMES ANDREWS, 27, clerk. He previously worked for another company, which has promised to forward all his tax forms to him.
HAROLD BASSETT, 52, caretaker. He also works as a self-employed interior decorator at weekends, but his income from that job is very low.

1 Are you going to fill in the form? Explain your action by reference to the text.
2 If you fill in Section A, are you going to answer 'Yes' or 'No' to the last question?
3 If you have filled in Section A, what are you going to do when you have completed it?
4 If you fill in Section B, is the answer to the last question A or B?
5 What are you going to do when you have completed Section B?

Exercise 3

● **alone (*adv., NOT adj.*) lonely, only (*adj./adv.*), single, unique**

Choose the correct word to complete the following.

1 He lives ¹_____ in a very ²_____ house in the country, miles from the nearest village. He must be ³_____ himself, because he has very few friends. ⁴_____ he knows why he has chosen to live there. The ⁵_____ people he ever sees are a few farmers. He's never offered a ⁶_____ reason for his behaviour. Of course, he was an ⁷_____ child, with no brothers and sisters, so he's used to being ⁸_____, and it looks as if he'll spend his life as a ⁹_____ man. He'll never marry.

2 *A:* I'd like a _____ room, please.
    B: Yes, sir. Room 269 is free. It's the best room in the hotel. The view is _____. You'll never see anything like it.

Correspondence

Introductory exercise

The letters below use abbreviations for a
number of states in the USA: Conn.
(Connecticut), N.Y. (New York), Ark. (Arkansas),
Va. (Virginia).

*Find out what the following abbreviations stand
for.*

1	Co.	8	Ltd.
2	c/o	9	N.B.
3	dept.	10	P.S.
4	e.g.	11	P.T.O.
5	etc.	12	R.S.V.P.
6	i.e.	13	trans.
7	I.O.U.	14	vol.

Mix-up by mail

West Cornwall, Conn.   1
November 2, 1948

Miss Alma Winege,
The Charteriss Publishing Co.,
132 East What Street,
New York, N.Y.

DEAR MISS WINEGE:

Your letter of October 25th, which you sent to me **in care of** The
Homestead, Hot Springs, Ark., has been forwarded to my home
in West Cornwall, Conn., by The Homestead, Hot Springs, Va.
As you know, Mrs. Thurber and I sometimes visit this Virginia
resort, but we haven't been there for more than a year. I explained
to Mr. Cluffman, when I last called at your offices, that all mail
was to be sent to me at West Cornwall until further notice. If and
when I go to The Homestead, I will let you know in advance.
Meanwhile, I suggest that you remove from your files all
addresses of mine except the West Cornwall one. Another
publishing firm recently sent a letter to me at 65 West 11th Street,
an address I vacated in the summer of 1930. It would not come as a
surprise to me if your firm, or some other publishers, **wrote me** in

in care of: care of, c/o (UK)

wrote me: wrote to me (UK)

care of my mother at 568 Oak Street, Columbus, Ohio. I was thirteen years old when we lived there, back in 1908.

As for the contents of your letter of the 25th, I did not order thirty-six copies of Peggy Peckham's book "Grandma Was a Nudist." I trust that you have not shipped these books to me in care of The Homestead, Hot Springs, Ark., or anywhere else.

Sincerely yours,
J. THURBER

Miss Alma Winege,
The Charteriss Publishing Co.,
132 East What Street,
New York, N.Y.

2

DEAR MISS WINEGE:

In this morning's mail I received a card from the Grand Central branch of the New York Post Office informing me that a package of books had been delivered to me at 410 East 57th Street. I am enclosing the notification card, since these must be the thirty-six copies of "Grandma Was a Nudist." I have not lived at 410 East 57th Street since the **fall** of 1944. Please see to it that this address is removed from your files.

fall: autumn (UK)

Sincerely yours,
J. THURBER

THE CHARTERISS PUBLISHING COMPANY
NEW YORK, N.Y.

3

November 5, 1948

Mr. James M. Thurber,
West Cornwall, Conn.

DEAR MR. THURBER:

I am dreadfully sorry about the mix-up over Miss Peckham's book. We have been pretty much upset around here since the departure of Mr. Peterson and Mr. West, but I still cannot understand from what file our shipping department got your address as 165 West 11th Street. I have removed the 57th Street address from the files and also the Arkansas address and I trust that we will not disturb your tranquillity further up there in Cornwall. It must be lovely this time of year in Virginia and I envy you and Mrs. Thurber. Have a lovely time at The Homestead.

Sincerely yours,
ALMA WINEGE

Columbus, Ohio   4
November 16, 1948

Mr. James M. Thurber,
West Cornwall, Conn.

DEAR MR. THURBER:

I have decided to come right out with the little problem that was accidentally dumped in my lap yesterday. I hope you will forgive me for what happened, and perhaps you can suggest what I should do with the books. There are three dozen of them and, unfortunately, they arrived when my little son Donald was alone downstairs. By the time I found out about the books, he had torn off the wrappings and had built a **cute** little house out of them. I have placed them all on a shelf out of his reach while awaiting word as to where to send them. I presume I could ship them to you C.O.D. if I can get somebody to wrap them properly.

cute: attractive, charming (UK)

Sincerely yours,
CLARA EDWARDS
(MRS J. C.)

From *Alarms and Diversions* by James Thurber (abridged)

Exercise 1

For the first time, there are four choices in multiple-choice questions here, as in the Cambridge FCE examination, but you should follow the same procedure as before.

Compare each of these statements with the letters and decide which are true and which are false. Only **one** *answer is correct in each case.*

1 When did Mr Thurber last live at the following addresses:
   The Homestead, Hot Springs, Arkansas;
   The Homestead, Hot Springs, Virginia;
   410 East 57th St., New York;
   165 West 11th St., New York?
   a This year.
   b Last year.
   c Some years before.
   d Never.

2 Miss Winege's company must originally have sent
   a some books he ordered to an address in Arkansas.
   b some books he ordered to an address in New York.
   c someone else's books to an address in Arkansas.
   d someone else's books to an address in New York.

3 In Miss Winege's opinion, the confusion has been caused mainly by
   a changes in the staff.
   b Mr Thurber having more than one address.
   c the fact that he ordered a different book.
   d his reference to the files.

4 She has obviously not read his letters carefully because she
   a thinks he wants her to send 36 books to Columbus, Ohio.
   b has removed his present address from the files.
   c seems to think he is going to Virginia.
   d told the shipping department he was at a New York address.

Exercise 2

*Give brief answers to these questions. Look
back to the letters to discover the answers.*
1   What do you suppose Mrs Edwards's address
    in Columbus, Ohio, is?
2   How do you imagine the company got hold of
    it?
3   What did they deliver to her?
4   Apparently, the address on the books was
    different from that on the outside of the
    parcel, otherwise Mrs Edwards would not
    have written to Mr Thurber. Where were the
    books addressed to?

Exercise 3

*Find words or phrases in the letters that are
similar in meaning to the following. The
number in brackets indicates the letter where
the word or phrase is to be found.*
1   sent (2 alternatives) (1)
2   left (1)
3   peace and quiet (3)
4   dropped unexpectedly (4)
5   suppose (4)

Exercise 4

● **explain, remark, say, talk, tell**

*Use each verb, **at least once**, in the correct
form to complete the following.*
1   'It's a nice day,' he _____. (2 possibilities)
2   We _____ about the weather for half an
    hour.
3   He asked me what my name was so I
    _____ him.
4   She _____ the children a story before they
    went to bed.
5   'The reason why we sent you the wrong
    books is that our files are not in very good
    order,' she _____. (2 possibilities)
6   '_____ him to wait outside,' I _____.
7   I'm afraid I can't _____ you when he'll be
    back.
8   When he _____ the situation to me, I
    understood immediately.
9   Some claim that they can't _____ the
    difference between margarine and butter. I'd
    be surprised if they could _____ the time!
10 Why did you _____ that to her? It was a
    very unkind remark.

Archaeology

Introductory exercise

*Before looking at the passage below, answer
these questions.*

1 Whereabouts in your body are your: *a* heart;
b lungs; *c* stomach; *d* throat; *e* tongue? What
purpose do they serve?

2 Name an item of clothing that might be made
of: *a* cotton; *b* leather; *c* linen; *d* silk; *e* wool.

Egyptian mummy-making

Mummy-making was big business in
ancient Egypt and became one of its
most perfected crafts. Originally bodies
were preserved by being buried in the
5 sand   –   thus   maintaining   the
individual's identity beyond the grave.
But as the era of the Pharaohs evolved,
so too did a desire to keep bodies in
sealed tombs beyond the reach of
10 predators, and the craft developed to
emulate the natural powers of the
desert.

The 'golden age' of mummy-making
was around 1,000 BC, by which time
15 even the brain could be removed, via
the nose. Next an incision was made in
the left side and the rest of the **viscera**
drawn out, leaving only the heart. The
empty abdominal cavity was then
20 rinsed with oils or palm wine and coated
with liquid **resins**.

The   extraction   of   the   water,
comprising about three-quarters of the
human body, remains a mummy-
25 maker's secret, but it is thought that the
body   was   packed   in   dry   *natron*,
containing sodium bicarbonate and
sodium chloride, which drew off the
liquid in 35 to 40 days. Finally the
30 dessicated body was bulked out with

padding, painted to simulate life and
wrapped in linen bandages.

In 1912 Sir Grafton Elliot Smith, a
British   anthropologist,   aired   the
35 possibility that the exhibition and study
of   mummies   might   give   rise   to
accusations of sacrilege. However, he
consoled   himself: 'Having   these
valuable   historic   documents   in   our
40 possession,' he said, 'it is surely our
duty   to   read   them   as   fully   and   as
carefully as possible.'

From *Autopsy on an Ancient Mummy* by
Hamilton Ford in the *Sunday Telegraph
Magazine* (abridged)

viscera: internal organs, especially
intestines
resins: sticky substances

Exercise 1

Choose the most likely meaning of these words or phrases in the context of the passage.

1 **drew off** (line 28): *a* pulled out (like a tooth) *b* removed gradually by drying out
2 **desiccated** (line 30): *a* dried *b* empty
3 **bulked out** (line 30): *a* made more attractive *b* filled out with packing
4 **aired** (line 34): *a* put forward in the open air *b* raised in public
5 **give rise to** (line 36): *a* lift up *b* be the cause of

Exercise 2

Choose the correct answer, a, b, c or d. Only **one** *answer is correct in each case.*

1 The main reason for the development of the art of making mummies was
   a to find a satisfactory method of preserving bodies.
   b to make them look attractive.
   c to protect bodies from robbers.
   d to keep them in a good state of preservation in a tomb.
2 As part of their preparations, mummy-makers
   a removed all the organs of the body.
   b coated the body with a sticky substance.
   c cleaned the inside of the body carefully.
   d made a cut in the face to remove the brain.
3 Modern anthropologists do not fully understand how
   a the brain was removed from the body.
   b the body was made to look lifelike after death.
   c the water was drawn off from the body.
   d the process of mummy-making developed.
4 Sir Grafton Elliot Smith's attitude towards displaying and studying mummies was that it was
   a irreligious.
   b a consolation for anthropologists' hard work.
   c necessary in the interests of science.
   d an insult to the dead.

Exercise 3

Up to now, you have done a number of exercises finding words and phrases that have a similar meaning to those in the text. True synonyms rarely exist in English, however, and in order to expand your comprehension of the use of words in the language further, it is necessary to begin to understand from the context why the writer has chosen one word and not another.

Use a good English dictionary (e.g. The Advanced Learner's Dictionary of Current English *(OUP) or* The Longman Dictionary of Contemporary English) *to check why the writer preferred the first word (used in the passage) to the second, which would be less precise.*

1   **crafts** (line 3) — techniques
2   **identity** (line 6) — personality
3   **grave** (line 6) — tomb
4   **era** (line 7) — age
5   **sealed** (line 9) — closed
6   **tombs** (line 9) — graves
7   **emulate** (line 11) — copy
8   **age** (line 13) — era
9   **incision** (line 16) — cut
10 **drawn out** (line 18) — drawn off
11 **rinsed** (line 20) — washed
12 **coated** (line 20) — covered
13 **drew off** (line 28) — drew out
14 **simulate** (line 31) — imitate

History

Introductory exercise

Before looking at the passage below, find answers to the following.
Can you name: *a* five British monarchs; *b* five Presidents of the United States; *c* five leaders of the Soviet Union?

The Prince of Wales in Paris (1855)

The Prince longed for independence, to know more of life beyond the walls of **Buckingham Palace** and the terraces of **Windsor**, to escape from the suffocating confines of his parents' court. When he was thirteen, in August 1855, he went to Paris with them on a state visit to Napoleon III. Lord Clarendon, the Foreign Secretary, who was instructed to keep an eye on him and to tell him how to behave, thought that the Queen's severity was 'very injudicious'.

For his own part, the Prince had never enjoyed himself more than he did in Paris; and he left it with obvious regret, looking intently all around him, 'as though anxious to lose nothing' of his last moments there. He had been intoxicated by the excitement of their welcome. He never forgot the fireworks at the Versailles ball; nor kneeling down in his **Highland dress** beside his mother to say a prayer at the tomb of Napoleon I; nor how he had hero-worshipped the romantic and mysterious Emperor to whom he had confided one afternoon as they drove round Paris together, 'I should like to be your son.'

He adored the Empress Eugénie, and he pleaded with her to let him and his sister stay behind for a few days on their own. The Empress replied that she was afraid that the Queen and Prince Albert could not do without them. 'Not do without us!' the Prince protested. 'Don't fancy that, for there are six more of us at home, and they don't want *us*.'

Buckingham Palace, Windsor, Osborne, Balmoral: royal palaces in Britain

Highland dress: The prince must have worn a kilt.

He really felt it to be true. When they got home he was sent away immediately to
Osborne with his tutors to make up for the lessons he had missed while he had been in
20 France. 'Poor Bertie' was 'pale and trembling' when his mother and father took leave of
him, the Queen recorded in her journal. 'The poor dear child' was 'much affected' at the
prospect of this 'first long separation'. But whether the Prince's emotion was due, as the
Queen thought, to his sadness at parting from his parents, or, as we may suppose more
likely, to his dread of returning to the **unremitting grind** of his lessons, it was certain
25 that once he had gone the Queen did not much miss him. As she confessed to the Queen
of Prussia that autumn, 'Even here (at **Balmoral**) when Albert is often away all day long,
I find no special pleasure in the company of the elder children . . . and only very
occasionally do I find the rather intimate intercourse with them either easy or agreeable.'
When they were naughty she found them intolerable, and was insistent that they be
30 punished even more severely than their father would have approved.

> **unremitting grind:** Lessons were hard work for the Prince, and even when he had a holiday, he had to make up for what he had missed.

From *Edward VII* by Christopher Hibbert (abridged)

Exercise 1

Decide on the probable meaning of these words or phrases in the context of the passage.

1 **suffocating confines** (lines 2–3): literally, 'choking limits', but why did the Prince feel unable to breathe, and what kind of limits?
2 **keep an eye on** (line 5): watch, but with what purpose?
3 **intoxicated** (line 9): It cannot mean 'drunk'. What other state would have made the Prince lose control of himself to some extent?
4 **do without** (line 16): *a* act without *b* manage without
5 **make up for** (line 19): *a* compensate for *b* add up

Exercise 2

Choose the correct answer, a, b, c or d. Only one answer is correct in each case.

1 The Prince's visit to Paris
   a allowed him to do exactly as he liked at last.
   b gave him the chance to get away from his parents all the time.
   c was something he always remembered.
   d was the cause of his regret on leaving home.
2 The Prince
   a thought the dead Napoleon I was a hero.
   b was very fond of the Emperor and Empress.
   c would like to have been French.
   d enjoyed himself because all the celebrations were in his honour.

3 The cause of disagreement between the Empress and the Prince was that
   a he wanted to stay in France on his own.
   b she knew the Queen and Prince Albert were lonely.
   c she thought he would be needed at home.
   d she did not want him to stay any longer.
4 The Prince was probably sorry to say goodbye to his parents because
   a he wished he were still in France.
   b he did not want to be separated from them.
   c he was in a poor state of health.
   d he hated the idea of going back to the schoolroom.
5 The Queen's attitude towards Bertie and his sister was that she
   a was unhappy when they were away from home.
   b found it difficult to get on with them.
   c found them a consolation in her husband's absence.
   d thought Prince Albert was too strict with them.

Exercise 3

Find words or phrases in the passage that are similar in meaning to the following. The number in brackets indicates the paragraph where the word or phrase is to be found.

1 unwise (1)
2 with great concentration (2)
3 imagine (3)
4 said goodbye to (4)
5 wrote down (4)

Exercise 4

Use a dictionary to check why the writer preferred the first word (used in the passage) to the second, and what additional meaning he intended to convey in this way.

1   **longed for** (line 1) — wanted
2   **confided** (line 12) — told
3   **adored** (line 14) — loved
4   **pleaded** (line 14) — asked
5   **protested** (line 17) — replied
6   **confessed** (line 25) — explained

Exercise 5

● **A   emotional, excited, exciting, impressed, impressive**

Choose the correct word to complete the following.

1   The Prince was _____ by the welcome they received in Paris.
2   He thought the fireworks at the Versailles ball were _____.
3   The simple ceremony at the tomb of Napoleon I was _____.
4   The Prince was very much _____ by the Emperor.
5   His _____ parting from his parents was probably not so for the reasons his mother imagined.

● **B   afraid, anxious, curious, worried**

Choose the correct word to complete the following.

The Prince was ¹_____ to know more of life outside his home. When he arrived in Paris, he was ²_____ and asked Lord Clarendon hundreds of questions. He would have liked to stay there longer, but the Empress was ³_____ his mother would be ⁴_____ (2 possibilities) about him, so he had to return. His relationship with his parents was unhappy. He knew they were ⁵_____ about his inability to learn, but he was ⁶_____ of his father and ⁷_____ to confide in his mother. The Queen's attitude was ⁸_____; she never forgave him for not being like his father.

Lexical Progress Test 4

You must choose the word or phrase which best completes each sentence. For each question, 1 to 25, indicate the correct answer, A, B, C or D. The time for the test is 20 minutes.

1   He had a cold and couldn't go to the party, so I bought him a cake to make up for his _____.
    A depression B disappointment C disillusion D disgust

2   I _____ you wouldn't drop your cigarette ash on the carpet!
    A claim B expect C want D wish

3   They all _____ their flags when the President drove past.
    A put B rocked C shook D waved

4   He won a gold medal at the Olympic _____.
    A Displays B Games C Plays D Sports

5   He _____ the job he was offered, because the pay wasn't good enough.
    A got away with B put off C turned down D turned over

6   She _____ the letter and put it in an envelope.
    A bent B folded C turned over D wrapped

7   Apart from his salary, he has a private _____ from investments.
    A benefit B earning C income D wage

8   The letters BBC _____ for British Broadcasting Corporation.
    A hold up B make up for C set out D stand for

9   I _____ this delightful old book quite by chance in my father's library.
    A came across B drew out C pulled off D went in for

10 His firm are expecting to make a big _____ this year.
    A benefit B profit C wage D winning

11 He _____ for his bad behaviour at the party.
    A apologised B excused C forgave D pardoned

12 _____ men and women pay higher taxes than those who are married.
    A Alone B Lonely C Only D Single

13 He isn't interested in what happens to you. It doesn't _____ to him.
    A care B depend C matter D mind

14 Would you mind _____ to me how the trouble started?
    A explaining B remarking C talking D telling

15 We are sorry your train is late. British Railways _____ the delay.
    A pities B regrets C resents D respects

16 The customs inspector examined the _____ of his case.
    A contents B filling C goods D insides

17 She dealt with all the reporters' questions very calmly. It was a most _____ performance.
    A embarrassing B emotional C impressed D impressive

18 I'm _____ I don't know what time she will be home.
    A afraid B anxious C troubled D worried

19 What's the _____ rainfall in Barcelona in March?
    A average B general C medium D middle

20 You're the _____ person who's ever understood me.
    A alone B lonely C only D unique

21 You've never _____ me about your experiences in Africa.
    A described B explained C said D told

22 I couldn't get any roses, so I bought tulips _____.
    A as well B else C instead D otherwise

23 That's the hotel I always _____ at in London.
    A keep B remain C rest D stay

24 You must _____ up for your rights; otherwise, the employers will get their own way, as usual.
    A call B draw C hang D stand

25 The river is so _____ near here that you can cross it on foot.
    A flat B narrow C shallow D straight

Test Papers

The papers are divided into two parts, Section A and Section B. For each question you answer correctly in Section A you gain **one** mark; for each question you answer correctly in Section B you gain **two** marks. No marks are deducted for wrong answers, so you should **always** try to answer the questions.

Test 1

Section A

In this section you must choose the word or phrase which best completes each sentence. For each question, 1–25, indicate the correct answer, A, B, C or D. The time for the whole test is one hour. You should not spend more than 20 minutes on this section.

1 I'm writing to _____ for the post you advertised yesterday.
   A apply B appoint C introduce D suggest

2 British Airways _____ the departure of Flight 123 to Palma.
   A advertises B advises C announces D notices

3 I don't _____ what you think. I'll do as I like.
   A care B concern C matter D occupy

4 Their prompt action prevented the fire from _____.
   A flowing B scattering C spilling D spreading

5 It's a good area for shopping. All the shops are within easy _____.
   A approach B arrival C neighbourhood D reach

6 The _____ of the clock moved slowly towards midnight.
   A arms B figures C fingers D hands

7 When it started to rain, they took shelter in a _____ hut.
   A close B near C nearby D nearly

8 They _____ their children by giving them everything they wanted.
   A damaged B spoilt C upset D wasted

9 Our dog has been _____ by a car.
   A hit down B knocked down C put down D run in

10 The company's poor results are likely to _____ people from making investments.
   A decrease B discourage C disturb D reduce

11 Have you _____ the tickets for the theatre tomorrow?
   A booked B engaged C paid D preserved

12 He's got a much better _____ now, in an advertising agency.
   A duty B employment C job D work

13 New students must _____ in classes before the term begins.
   A enrol B enter C join D put down

14 I told you that if we left the children on their own, they'd make a terrible _____.
   A damage B destruction C mess D nuisance

15 It's a good dog. It won't do you any _____.
   A bite B harm C hurt D pain

16 The main purpose in keeping fit is to feel more pleasure in being _____.
   A alive B conscious C live D lively

17 Someone from the Ministry of Education is coming to _____ our classes.
   A control B inspect C look on D overlook

18 I've found a marvellous _____ for curried chicken.
   A course B prescription C receipt D recipe

95

19 They all _____ their flags when the
President drove past.
A put *B* rocked *C* shook *D* waved

20 At the end of the game, the crowd _____
out of the ground.
A dropped *B* fell *C* left *D* poured

21 He was standing outside the gate, _____
on his bicycle.
A bending *B* bowing *C* leaning *D* sloping

22 I left home so late that I _____ had time to
catch the train.
A at least *B* just *C* nearly *D* scarcely

23 What's the _____ rainfall in Barcelona in
March?
A average *B* general *C* medium *D* middle

24 When I last saw him, he was _____ a
motorcycle.
A conducting *B* driving *C* guiding *D* riding

25 I'd like a packet of razor _____, please.
A blades *B* cuts *C* leaves *D* metals

Section B

*In this section you will find after each of the
passages a number of questions or unfinished
statements about the passage, each with four
suggested answers or ways of finishing. You
must choose the one which you think fits best.
For each question, 26 to 40, indicate the letters
A, B, C or D.*

● **First Passage**

For some time the Princess had been aware that
the Queen, though still extremely fond of her, had
been increasingly critical of her behaviour, and
that she strongly disapproved of the way she and
the Prince had spent so much time travelling
about when they should have been quietly
awaiting the birth of a baby who might have been
expected to enter the world weighing more than
three and three-quarter pounds.

The Queen's letters to her daughter had
recently been full of complaints about her
daughter-in-law's failure to improve her mind and
her son's thoughtlessness. 'She never reads,' the
Queen wrote. 'I fear her education has been much
neglected and she cannot either write, or, I fear,
speak French well.' Nor did she write English
well, though she seemed to spend half her time
writing letters. Even worse than this, she was deaf
and everyone noticed it, which was a 'sad
misfortune'.

Now that the baby was born, there was further
trouble over his name. The grandmother insisted
that there could be no question of his not being
called Albert, with Victor as a second name; and
she told her youngest daughter, the six-year-old
Princess Beatrice, who in turn told Lady
Macclesfield, that this had been decided. When
the news reached the father, he was not in the
least pleased. 'I felt rather annoyed,' he
complained to the Queen, 'when told that you
had settled what our little boy was to be called
before I had spoken to you about it.' Nor did the
Prince altogether approve of the Queen's
suggestion that all his descendants must bear the
names of either Albert or Victoria, generation
after generation for ever, and that when he
himself succeeded to the throne he should be
known as 'King Albert Edward'. Against his will,
he agreed that there was 'no absolute reason why
it should not be so', but felt obliged to point out
that no English monarch had borne a double
name in the past.

In the end, however, the Queen had her way
and the baby's first two names were Albert
Victor, with Christian added in compliment to his
maternal grandfather and Edward after the
Queen's father, the Duke of Kent. From then on
his parents knew him as Eddy, though the Queen
did not. And as if upset by the disagreements
which his christening had produced, the baby
'roared all through the ceremony'; while the
mother, so the Queen noted, 'looked very ill, thin
and unhappy'.

26 The Queen
   A did not like her daughter-in-law much.
   B considered that the Princess was
   thoughtless and misled the Prince.
   C believed she should have let the Prince
   go out by himself.
   D made her responsible for the size of her
   grandson.

27 The Princess's greatest defect in the
Queen's eyes was that she
   A could not speak French.
   B never read books.
   C was obviously deaf.
   D wrote too many letters.

28 The Prince was annoyed with his mother
because

A she wanted his son to be called Albert.

B she announced that the matter was already decided.

C she told one of the court ladies about her plans for her grandson.

D she insisted on speaking to him about the little boy's names.

29 The Prince also argued with her because

A he did not think the name of Albert was appropriate for a king.

B no English king had ever been called Albert.

C he did not see why his parents' names should always be used in the family.

D he thought the laws of the country prevented a king from having two names.

30 In the end, the parents

A only gave the baby the names the Queen wanted.

B always called the baby Eddy in the Queen's presence.

C took no notice of the Queen's wishes at home.

D were unhappy at the christening because they had not been allowed to choose the names.

● **Second Passage**

Most shoplifters agree that the January sales offer wonderful opportunities for the hard-working thief. With the shops so crowded and the staff so busy, it does not require any extraordinary talent to help yourself to one or two little things and escape unnoticed. It is known, in the business, as 'hoisting'.

But the hoisting game is not what it used to be. Even at the height of the sales, shoplifters today never know if they are being watched by one of those evil little balls that hang from the ceilings of so many department stores above the most desirable goods.

As if that was not trouble enough for them, they can now be filmed at work and obliged to attend a showing of their performance in court.

Selfridges was the first big London store to install closed-circuit videotape equipment to watch its sales floors. In October last year the store won its first court case for shoplifting using as evidence a videotape clearly showing a couple stealing dresses. It was an important test case

which encouraged other stores to install similar equipment.

When the balls, called sputniks, first made an appearance in shops it was widely believed that their only function was to frighten shoplifters. Their somewhat ridiculous appearance, the curious holes and red lights going on and off, certainly made the theory believable.

It did not take long, however, for serious shoplifters to start showing suitable respect. Soon after the equipment was in operation at Selfridges, store detective Brian Chadwick was sitting in the control room watching a woman secretly putting bottles of perfume into her bag.

'As she turned to go,' Chadwick recalled, 'she suddenly looked up at the 'sputnik' and stopped. She could not possibly have seen that the camera was trained on her because it is completely hidden, but she must have had a feeling that I was looking at her.

'For a moment she paused, then she returned to the counter and started putting everything back. When she had finished, she opened her bag towards the camera to show it was empty and hurried out of the store.'

31 January is a good month for shoplifters because

A they don't need to wait for staff to serve them.

B they don't need any previous experience as thieves.

C there are so many people in the stores.

D there are more goods in the shops.

32 The sputniks hanging from the ceilings are intended

A as an amusing kind of decoration.

B to make films that can be used in evidence.

C to frighten shoplifters by their appearance.

D to be used as evidence against shoplifters.

33 The case last October was important because

A the store got the dresses back.

B it repaid the investment on the equipment.

C other shops found out about the equipment.

D the kind of evidence supplied was accepted.

34 The woman stealing perfume
   A guessed what the sputnik was for.
   B was frightened by its shape.
   C could see the camera filming her.
   D knew that the detective had seen her.
35 The woman's action before leaving the store shows that she
   A was sorry for what she had done.
   B was afraid she would be arrested.
   C decided she didn't want what she had picked up.
   D wanted to prove she had not intended to steal anything.
36 If an accident has occurred, the safety representative has the right to
   A carry out an inspection every three months.
   B carry out inspections more frequently.
   C consult management about more frequent inspections.
   D carry out an inspection immediately.
37 If you saw something fall off a shelf and just miss another worker, you should
   A call a meeting to investigate it.
   B report it to the management immediately.
   C report it to the safety representative.
   D leave him to report it himself.

38 Union safety representatives should reach an agreement with the management so that they can
   A work together on investigating complaints.
   B decide on accident procedures.
   C reach the scene of the accident as soon as possible.
   D get special treatment for union members.
39 When recording an accident, safety representatives should
   A try to find out who caused the accident.
   B try to find out what caused the accident.
   C try to put the blame on the management.
   D prevent witnesses from speaking to the management.
40 While making enquiries, safety representatives should
   A make sure that no evidence is moved.
   B ask witnesses to sign their statements.
   C inform the factory inspector personally.
   D get witnesses to take photographs as evidence.

Labour Research Department

the information service for trade unionists
more information from:
LRD 78 Blackfriars Road London SE1

Preventing accidents

Clearly a major way to prevent accidents before they occur is for the safety representative to carry out regular and effective inspections of the workplace. Recognised safety representatives have the following legal rights.

- To carry out a formal inspection every three months (or more frequently if agreed with management);

- To carry out an additional inspection:
  - when a notifiable accident has occurred;
  - when there has been a dangerous occurrence;
  - when a notifiable disease has been contracted;
  - when there has been a change in working conditions;
  - when new information becomes available concerning hazards;
- To investigate members' complaints;

- To investigate on the safety reps' own initiative.

Near misses

All union members should be encouraged to report 'near misses' that happen to themselves or others. Near misses are events such as slipping on wet floors, items falling off shelves and just missing people, loose guards on machinery, fires that are quickly put out and so on that could have injured people but which, by luck, do not. Reporting and acting upon such events may prevent a serious accident in the future.

When an accident happens

Union safety reps should ensure that they have an agreement with management to ensure that they are informed as soon as possible of all accidents. In addition they should ensure that their own union members, and any others they represent, know the importance of informing them of any accident or near-miss, however trivial. On hearing of an accident they should follow these procedures.

- Go straight to the accident.

- Make sure it is safe to approach.

- Make sure anyone injured is receiving attention.

- Insist that nothing is removed or altered until enquiries are complete.

- Check the accident is recorded in the accident book and that the record is not concerned with blaming the victim but is an accurate description which will be an aid to accident prevention in the future.

- Take statements from the injured person(s) if possible and other witnesses (in confidence if required: this is your legal right). Remind witnesses they do not, by law, have to give statements to the management.

- Check that the factory inspector has been informed if required by law.

- Sketch accident area, take photographs if possible, samples of defective equipment, chemicals, etc. if required; get witnesses to authenticate same if possible.

Test 2

Section A

In this section you must choose the word or phrase which best completes each sentence. For each question, 1–25, indicate the correct answer, A, B, C or D. The time for the whole test is one hour. You should not spend more than 20 minutes on this section.

1   I'd be _____ if you would let me have her address.
    A graceful *B* grateful *C* pleasant *D* thanked

2   Why are you looking at me with that strange _____?
    A appearance *B* expression *C* sight *D* watch

3   Who's left the tap running? There's a _____ of water on the floor.
    A bucket *B* heap *C* pool *D* stain

4   The first _____ of the play did not go very well.
    A action *B* performance *C* show *D* time

5   They've built a _____ of very attractive houses near the station.
    A file *B* procession *C* queue *D* row

6   I'm afraid the lift is out of _____. We'll have to walk.
    A function *B* order *C* repair *D* work

7   Do you like my new car? It's the latest _____.
    A brand *B* mark *C* model *D* pattern

8   I'll solve the problem. Just _____ everything to me.
    A lay *B* lead *C* leave *D* let

9   You're not serious, are you? I thought you were _____.
    A amusing *B* enjoying *C* joking *D* tricking

10 He's always nervous when he has to make a _____.
    A discussion *B* pronunciation *C* speech *D* talk

11 The boat turned over and sank to the _____.
    A base *B* basis *C* bottom *D* ground

12 It was an accident. He didn't do it on _____.
    A appointment *B* decision *C* intention *D* purpose

13 The elephant fell into a _____ the hunters had set.
    A track *B* trap *C* trick *D* trunk

14 There are a number of arguments you must take into _____.
    A account *B* mind *C* scale *D* thought

15 We had very bad weather on holiday. We enjoyed ourselves, _____.
    A although *B* however *C* in spite *D* therefore

16 We must _____ up to the problems ahead of us.
    A face *B* glance *C* see *D* stare

17 I've washed up and _____ the floors. Now I'm going out.
    A dusted *B* scraped *C* spread *D* swept

18 People always say the children _____ me, but I think they're more like my husband.
    A appear as *B* follow on *C* keep on *D* take after

19 As in most popular romances, the hero and heroine quarrel, but get married _____.
    A at least *B* in the end *C* lastly *D* on the end

20 He _____ for his bad behaviour at the party.
    A apologised *B* excused *C* forgave *D* pardoned

21 Hello! I never expected you to _____ to the meeting.
    A arrive *B* bring round *C* present *D* turn up

22 I've been _____ by a bee, and it's very painful.
    A bitten *B* picked *C* scratched *D* stung

23 You've never _____ me about your experiences in Africa.
    A described *B* explained *C* said *D* told

24 The concert was very disappointing. It didn't _____ our expectations.
    A live up to *B* overcome *C* run over *D* show off

25 He took out a big _____ of keys, and opened the door.
    A branch *B* bunch *C* group *D* packet

Section B

In this section you will find after each of the passages a number of questions or unfinished statements about the passage, each with four suggested answers or ways of finishing. You must choose the one which you think fits best. For each question, 26 to 40, indicate the letter A, B, C or D.

● **First Passage**

Sixteen years ago, Eileen Doyle's husband, an engineer, took his four children up an early morning cup of tea, packed a small case and was never seen or heard of again. Eileen was astonished and in a state of despair. They had been a happy family and, as far as she knew, there had been nothing wrong with their marriage.

Every day of the year a small group of men and women quietly pack a few belongings and without so much as a note or a goodbye close the front door for the last time, leaving their debts, their worries and their confused families behind them.

Last year, more than 1,200 men and nearly as many women were reported missing from home — the highest in 15 years. Many did return home within a year, but others rejected the past completely and are now living a new life somewhere under a different identity.

To those left behind this form of desertion is a terrible blow to their pride and self-confidence. Even the finality of death might be preferable. At least it does not imply rejection or failure. Worse than that, people can be left with an unfinished marriage, not knowing whether they will have to wait seven years before they are free to start a fresh life.

Clinical psychologist Paul Brown believes most departures of this kind to be well planned rather than impulsive. 'It's typical of the kind of personality which seems able to ignore other people's pain and difficulties. Running away, like killing yourself, is a highly aggressive act. By creating an absence the people left behind feel guilty, upset and empty.'

The Salvation Army's Investigation Department have a 70 per cent success rate in tracking missing people down. According to Lt. Col. Bramwell Pratt, head of the department, men and women run away for very different

reasons though lack of communication is often the biggest motive. 'The things that disturb a man's personality are problems like being tied up in debt, or serious worries about work. And some women make impossible demands on their husbands. Women usually leave for more obvious reasons but fear is at the root of it. Men are more often prepared to give their marriage another try than women, but we are aware that, for some wives, it would be a total impossibility to return after the way they've been treated.'

26 When her husband left home, Eileen Doyle
   A could not forgive him for taking the children.
   B had been expecting it to happen for some time.
   C could not understand why.
   D blamed herself for what had happened.

27 Most people who leave their families
   A do so without warning.
   B do so because of their debts.
   C come back immediately.
   D change their names.

28 The man or woman left behind usually
   A admits responsibility for the situation.
   B wishes the person who has left were dead.
   C feels embarrassed and useless.
   D knows he or she cannot get married again for seven years.

29 Paul Brown regards leaving home in such circumstances as
   A an act of despair.
   B an act of selfishness.
   C the result of a sudden decision.
   D a kind way of drawing the partner's attention to problems.

30 The Salvation Army believe that
   A men and women leave their families for similar reasons.
   B men's reasons are more understandable than women's.
   C women never want to give men another chance.
   D women are often afraid to start the marriage again.

● Second Passage

The Government has almost doubled its spending on computer education in schools. Mr William Shelton, junior Education Minister, announced that the Microelectronics Education Programme (MEP) is to run for two more years with additional funding of at least £9 million.

The programme began in 1980, was originally due to end next year, and had a budget of £9 million. This has been raised in bits and pieces over the past year to £11 million. The programme will now run until March 1986, at a provisional cost of around £20 million.

MEP provides courses for teachers and develops computer programmes for classroom use of personal computers. It is run in partnership with a Department of Industry programme under which British-made personal computers are supplied to schools at half-price.

In that way, virtually every secondary school has been provided with at least one computer at a central cost to the taxpayer of under £5 million. The primary schools are now being supplied in a £9 million programme which got under way at the turn of the year.

But, as Mr Shelton admitted yesterday: 'It's no good having the computers without the right computer programmes to put into them and a great deal more is still needed.' Hence, MEP's new funds.

Mr Shelton said yesterday that MEP's achievements in curriculum development and teacher training had shown that the computer could be used in all courses.

About 15,000 secondary teachers have taken short courses in 'computer awareness' — that is a necessary part of the half-price computer offer — and training materials are now being provided for 50,000 primary teachers.

The reasoning behind MEP is that no child now at school can hope for a worthwhile job in the future economy unless he or she understands how to deal with computers — not in a vocational training sense, but in learning the general skill to extract the required information of the moment from the ever-spreading flood.

31 The original MEP programme was expected to
   A last two years and cost nine million pounds.
   B last four years and cost nine million pounds.
   C last two years and cost eleven million pounds.
   D last four years and cost eleven million pounds.

32 The main aim of MEP is to help curriculum development and
   A provide personal computers for schools.
   B arrange for cheap computers to be supplied to schools.
   C show teachers how to use personal computers.
   D train teachers to work with classes using computers.

33 Computers have now been introduced
   A in most secondary schools.
   B in all secondary schools.
   C in most primary schools, at half-price.
   D in most schools, at no expense to the taxpayer.

34 The additional grant of money being provided is mainly
   A part of the agreement to supply computers cheaply.
   B to develop further computer programmes for schools.
   C to train 50,000 primary teachers.
   D to provide courses for secondary teachers.

35 The reasons for the introduction of computers in schools is that
   A in future, all teaching will be done with computers.
   B computer programmers will have better jobs in future.
   C large numbers of people will have to be trained as computer programmers.
   D people will need to understand them to obtain information in their work.

Third Passage

SO YOU WANT TO STOP SMOKING

1 Think about stopping

The big question is: do you *really* want to stop? Because this is the key to success. Make up your mind you are going to stop, and you will. Lots of people have been surprised how easy it was to stop once they had really made up their minds.

To help you make your decision, think about what you gain by stopping.

Right away

- You will be free from an expensive and damaging habit.
- You'll have another £5 – £10 a week to spend.
- You'll smell fresher. No more bad breath, stained fingers or teeth.
- You'll be healthier and breathe more easily – for example, when you climb stairs or run for a bus.

Think of the money you'll save.

- And you'll be free of the worry that you may be killing yourself.

For the future

- You will lose your smoker's cough.
- You will suffer fewer colds and other infections.
- And you will avoid the dangers that smokers have to face.

Another ... 200 yards ... and ... I'll be home ...

About a quarter of young men who smoke will be killed before their time by tobacco.

Many people killed by smoking could have lived 10, 20, even 30 or more years longer. On average, people killed by smoking lose 10 to 15 years of their lives.

Among 1,000 young men who smoke, about 6 will be killed on the roads but about 250 will be killed before their time by tobacco.

Women who smoke when they are pregnant run a greater risk of miscarriage or of their baby being born premature or underweight.

If you stop smoking before you have got cancer or serious heart or lung disease from smoking, then you will avoid nearly all the risks of death or disability from smoking.

Family and friends

Once you stop smoking, your family and friends will gain too.

- They can enjoy fresher air.
- You'll be nicer to be with. Remember the slogan 'Kiss a non-smoker and taste the difference'.
- Children who live in smoke-free homes are much less likely to get colds and even pneumonia.
- If you don't smoke, your children are less likely to start.
- And although the main risk of smoking is to the smoker, non-smokers who live with a smoker have a higher chance of getting chest diseases.

For you, your family and friends, the benefits of stopping start on the day you stop smoking, and go on for good.

OH BOB DARLING! IT WOULD BE SO MUCH NICER IF YOU DIDN'T SMOKE ALL THE TIME.

The Health Education Council
Helping you to better health
78 New Oxford Street, London WC1A 1AH

---

36 The article suggests that the most effective way to give up smoking is to
   A say you are going to do so and believe it.
   B have a real wish to do so.
   C get help to make a decision.
   D think of all the money you are going to save.

37 If you give up smoking, you will immediately
   A stop coughing.
   B stop catching cold so often.
   C stop worrying about its effects.
   D be able to climb stairs easily and run after buses.

38 If you stop smoking before it is too late, you will
   A not die of the diseases smoking causes.
   B be much less likely to die before the age of 70.

   C add 10 to 15 years to your life.
   D have less chance of being killed on the roads.

39 The harmful effects of smoking
   A are limited to the smoker.
   B mainly affect young children.
   C are the result of the smoker kissing others.
   D are due to the atmosphere in the house.

40 If a father smokes heavily, his children
   A are more likely to smoke themselves.
   B are certain to get chest diseases.
   C are likely to be underweight at birth.
   D will be put off smoking when they grow up.

Test 3

Section A

In this section you must choose the word or phrase which best completes each sentence. For each question, 1–25, indicate the correct answer, A, B, C or D. The time for the whole test is one hour. You should not spend more than 20 minutes on this section.

1   I doubt if I can _____ a holiday this year.
    A afford B pay C pretend D spend
2   He'll never be a successful salesman. He's much too _____.
    A ashamed B embarrassed C shameful D shy
3   She was so upset that she _____ into tears.
    A broke B burst C fell D started
4   Unless you _____ 80% of the classes, you won't get a certificate.
    A assist B attend C follow D take place
5   People should be _____ to use their abilities to the maximum.
    A encouraged B favoured C supplied D supported
6   He's worked very hard and _____ a rise in salary.
    A belongs B deserves C owes D owns
7   I'm sorry we're late. We were _____ by the traffic.
    A held up B pulled up C put back D taken back
8   I can't _____ people singing out of tune.
    A hold B pass C stand D support
9   I thought his decision showed very good _____.
    A firmness B idea C judgement D opinion
10 She works as a _____ teacher, as well as at the Institute.
    A particular B personal C private D proper
11 _____ to write to Aunt Mary to thank her for her present.
    A Refer B Remember C Remind D Repeat
12 He's already apologised. There's no need to lose your _____.
    A condition B mood C sense D temper
13 When you've washed up, _____ the plates before you put them away.
    A clean B dust C sweep D wipe

14 See if you can take the bucket through the kitchen without _____ any of the water in it.
    A dropping B falling C sinking D spilling
15 He suffered _____ losses when his factory was burned down.
    A dear B hard C hardly D heavy
16 Moussaka is a very popular _____ in Greece.
    A cook B dish C menu D plate
17 We are sorry your train is late. British Railways _____ the delay.
    A pities B regrets C resents D respects
18 I'm afraid we'll have to _____ for a moment while I find the place in my notes.
    A arrest B hang C pause D resist
19 We're waiting until our correspondent _____ on the latest events in New York.
    A accounts B informs C reports D tells
20 The restaurant was _____ a country house, before it was converted.
    A at once B firstly C in time D originally
21 That's the hotel I always _____ at in London.
    A keep B remain C rest D stay
22 An enormous crowd was _____ outside the palace.
    A displaying B gathering C picking D surrounding
23 If we don't pay the bill, the gas will be _____.
    A cut off B pulled out C taken over D turned back
24 He shouldn't promise to help and then _____ us _____ at the last moment.
    A drop ... off B let ... down C put ... away D take ... back
25 It was spring, and the flowers were _____.
    A coming out B going out C growing up D raising

Section B

In this section you will find after each of the passages a number of questions or unfinished statements about the passage, each with four suggested answers or ways of finishing. You must choose the one which you think fits best. For each question, 26 to 40, indicate the letter A, B, C or D.

● **First Passage**

Since he was a child Don Cameron has been interested in anything which flies. He grew up on the outskirts of Glasgow and, as a student at Glasgow University, joined the University Air Squadron. Interest in the mechanics of movement, if not flight, was a family tradition. His grandfather was an engineer, who turned his hand to making model steam engines and boats.

Don Cameron's first job was at Bristol Aircraft, where he worked as an engineer. He then had jobs in the steelworks at Llanwern and for Rio-Tinto Zinc in Bristol, working with computers. In the mid-sixties, news of American experiments with hot air balloons crossed the Atlantic, and he and a couple of friends decided to build their own balloon. Probably the first hot air balloon in western Europe, they called it *The Bristol Belle*. Now there are 300 balloons in this country alone — and at least two-thirds of them have been made by the firm Don Cameron set up, Cameron Balloons.

At 40 he has already been halfway round the world by balloon. In 1972 he piloted the first hot-air balloon to cross the Swiss Alps; and later that year he took part in what he calls 'an odd expedition' to the Sahara Desert, with two balloons and a truck to carry the gas. He has crossed the Channel by balloon and even flown in the Arctic Circle in one. 'Before you fly there,' he remembers, 'you are told how to build igloos and survive in the snow. It's a lovely place to fly.'

'In the early days,' he recalls, 'I used to work night and day.' He looks down at his schedule for the next few days. It includes a drive to France to make a delivery, plus reading proofs of a ballooning handbook he has written. 'I still don't take it very easy,' he says. He started the business in the basement of the large Victorian house where he lives with his wife Kim and two children. Now Cameron Balloons has its own premises in an old church hall in Bristol, making about 150 balloons a year. They include specially designed balloons for advertising purposes. The firm exports all over the world and is setting up a factory in America, where balloons will be made for them under licence. The turnover is now around £500,000 a year and there is a staff of about 25.

26 Don Cameron's interest in flying
   A began at school.
   B began at university.
   C came from a wish to imitate his grandfather.
   D was the result of his professional experience.

27 He began working with balloons
   A as a relaxation from his work on aircraft.
   B as part of his job at the time.
   C as a hobby.
   D when he heard that some Americans had crossed the Atlantic in one.

28 Don Cameron's company
   A is the only one of its kind in Britain.
   B made the first balloon in Europe.
   C has made most of the balloons in Britain.
   D is now the largest in the world.

29 When he started his company, Don
   A spent most of his time on test flights.
   B was mainly interested in designing balloons for advertising.
   C worked hard, whereas now he relaxes.
   D built the balloons at home.

30 The success of Don's business can be measured by the fact that
   A he has made 150 of the balloons in Britain.
   B he now has enough orders to employ a number of people.
   C he delivers balloons to France.
   D he is going to move his factory to America.

● Second Passage

England's 400 HM Inspectors (Wales has its own force of 50) provide small teams to go into selected schools for a 3–5 day inspection according to size or type. This is sometimes because they have been criticised by parents, councillors or the Press. There may be other reasons: possibly a school is known for its particularly high standards, in which case the Inspectorate will wish to learn the secret and pass it on to the Minister concerned. Possibly, an informal inspector's visit had already dug up signs of trouble. This would certainly lead to a fuller inspection.

Schools cannot refuse to be inspected; nor can the inspectors order the dismissal of any member of staff. Teachers are not their concern. Teaching is. This is not to say that an awful teacher will be ignored. Remarks will certainly be made to the headmaster and chief education officer — but they will be verbal, not written.

So what is it that HM Inspectors do? For one thing, they will want to take a close look at the courses offered and what standards are achieved by pupils. They also compare teachers' qualifications with the subjects they teach. All too often teachers qualified in, say history, are forced to teach maths, where there is a shortage.

Examination results are also looked at carefully, as are the school's disciplinary arrangements, its accommodation (do pupils have to sit in the corridors or in mobile classrooms; are lavatories outside; does the roof leak when it rains?) and the textbooks and equipment used.

Before leaving the inspected school, HMI will give the head and local authority leader some indication of its findings, so the reports, which take some months to put together and print, do not come as a total surprise.

There are about 30,000 schools, colleges and polytechnics in England. Although there are only about 250 formal inspections a year, visits are far more numerous. Last year alone, three out of four secondary schools, one-quarter of all primary and middle schools, almost half of the special schools, 20 per cent of all independent schools and nine out of 10 further and higher education colleges were visited.

31 The Inspectors always visit schools
   A for the same number of days.
   B if a brief inspection suggests something is wrong.
   C if parents have complained about them.
   D if they hear that the school is doing very well.

32 When the teachers at a school are unsatisfactory
   A the school can prevent the inspectors from seeing them.
   B the inspectors make critical comments.
   C the inspectors send a report to the headmaster.
   D the inspectors have power to get rid of them.

33 The main reason why inspectors study teachers' qualifications is that
   A many teachers are not officially qualified.
   B some teachers refuse to teach unpopular subjects.
   C some teachers are not being employed appropriately.
   D headmasters often neglect certain subjects.

34 Inspectors' recommendations on schools
   A are immediately communicated in general terms.
   B are kept secret from the schools concerned until they are made public.
   C frequently come as a shock to headmasters.
   D take so long to appear that they are not very useful.

35 If you were a teacher in a secondary school in Britain, you would have been less likely to receive a visit from an inspector last year than if you worked in
   A a primary school.
   B a special school.
   C an independent school.
   D a further education college.

Essential Information for Motoring Abroad

Driving licence and International Driving Permit

It is recommended that you always carry your national driving licence with you when motoring abroad, even when an International Driving Permit is held. In most countries covered by 5-Star Service a visitor can drive a temporarily imported car for up to three months with a valid (not provisional) licence issued in the United Kingdom or Republic of Ireland, but must be 18 or over. The exceptions to this are Denmark, German Federal Republic, Greece, Iceland (where visitors must obtain temporary local driving permit from police), Luxembourg, Norway, Portugal, Tunisia and Turkey where visitors may drive at 17 (but see also IDP below). In Italy your licence must be accompanied by a translation which can be supplied by the AA. In Austria your UK driving licence is acceptable but language difficulties do occasionally give rise to misunderstandings which can generally be resolved by production of your passport.

The International Driving Permit is an internationally recognised document issued by the AA for a statutory fee to persons of 18 or over who hold a valid (not provisional) United Kingdom driving licence. It enables the holder to drive for a limited period in countries where their national licences are not recognised. The permit is compulsory in Algeria, Austria∗, Bulgaria, Czechoslovakia, Greece∗, Hungary, Morocco (locally registered hired vehicle), Spain (unless a certified Spanish translation of driving licence is obtained, although this is more expensive than an IDP) and Turkey (locally registered hired vehicles). It is recommended that all visitors to Finland (for locally registered hired vehicles), German Democratic Republic, Morocco, Poland, Tunisia, Turkey and the USSR obtain an IDP. The IDP may be obtained by a personal visit to any AA Travel Agency or Service Centre and producing your driving licence and a passport type photograph. Residents of the Republic of Ireland, Channel Islands and the Isle of Man should apply to their local AA office.
∗Required by Republic of Ireland licence holders only. ◢

Fire extinguishers

It is compulsory in Bulgaria, German Democratic Republic, Greece and USSR (and recommended in Iceland) for all vehicles to be equipped with fire extinguishers.

First-aid kit

It is compulsory in Austria, Bulgaria, Czechoslovakia, German Democratic Republic, Greece, USSR and Yugoslavia (and recommended in Iceland) for all vehicles to be equipped with a first-aid kit.

Hazard warning lights

Although hazard warning lights are normally acceptable their use can be prevented by accident damage or electrical failure and a warning triangle should always be carried. Therefore, hazard warning lights should not be used instead of the triangle but to complement it.
Note in *Czechoslovakia* any vehicle warning lights, other than those supplied with the vehicle as original equipment, must be made inoperative.

Insurance

Motor vehicle insurance is compulsory in all countries within the 5-Star Service area. Therefore, before taking a vehicle abroad you should contact your own insurers for their advice and to make sure that you are adequately covered. Insurance policies issued in the United Kingdom and Republic of Ireland automatically provide the minimum legal insurance requirements in some countries. However, as the level of legal cover varies from country to country, you are recommended to obtain an International Green Card of Insurance from your insurers to make sure that you enjoy the same measure of protection as you do in your country of residence. The Green Card is compulsory in Bulgaria, Greece, Iceland, Morocco, Poland, Portugal, Romania, Spain, Tunisia, Turkey and Yugoslavia. If you are involved in an accident you should notify your insurance company, by letter if possible, within 24 hours of the accident.

(This information is correct as of 10 August 1983.)

36 If you are travelling in Austria in your own car and hold a valid UK licence, you
    A must be over 18.
    B must have an International Driving Permit.
    C must carry an International Green Card of Insurance.
    D need not carry first-aid kit.

37 If you are travelling in Greece in your own car and hold a valid UK licence, you
    A must be over 18.
    B must have an International Driving Permit.
    C must carry an International Green Card of Insurance.
    D need not carry a first-aid kit.

38 When driving abroad, you should take a warning triangle because
    A hazard warning lights are not accepted in a number of countries.
    B hazard warning lights may not be usable in some circumstances.
    C hazard warning lights cannot be used in Czechoslovakia.
    D hazard warning lights should not be used together with a triangle.

39 The booklet states that drivers
    A should take out a UK or Irish insurance policy.
    B must take out a UK or Irish insurance policy.
    C should take out an International Green Card of Insurance.
    D must take out an International Green Card of Insurance.

40 The International Driving Permit is primarily intended
    A to be used instead of a national driving licence.
    B for drivers who are over 18.
    C for drivers who want to spend over three months abroad.
    D for drivers in countries where the driving licence is not accepted.

Appendix

Appendix

BACK *v.t. & i.* **back out (of)** Withdraw from (a scheme, agreement, etc.) †*He wants to back out of the contract.*

back up Support †*Ask him for a rise in salary. I'll back you up.*

BEAR *v.t. & i.* **bear up** Not show feelings of pain, despair † *Bear up! The worst is over now.* †*She has borne up bravely throughout her illness.*

BREAK *v.t. & i.* **break down 1** Stop, especially because of mechanical failure †*My car broke down, and I had to walk.* †*Negotiations have broken down.* **2** Collapse †*Her health broke down under the strain* †*She broke down when she heard the news* (i.e. She burst into tears).

break off 1 Stop speaking suddenly †*He broke off in the middle of a sentence and looked round.* **2** End (a relationship) suddenly †*He broke off his engagement to her the day before the wedding.*

BRING *v.t. & i.* **bring about** Cause (gradually) †*His kindness brought about a change in her attitude towards him.*

bring out Demonstrate (by examples) †*His book brings out the difficulties which face people beginning a new life in a strange country.*

bring up 1 Raise (a subject) †*The meeting was nearly over when he brought up the problem of the new wage rates.* **2** Rear a child †*Her parents died when she was very young, and she was brought up by her aunt and uncle.* †*What a well brought-up child!* (well-behaved, because of her parents' example, etc.)

CALL *v.t. & i.* **call for 1** Need, demand (frequently with object and verb in passive voice) †*Building a new bridge will call for a large sum of money.* †*The opposition leader called for an election (to be held).* **2** Collect †*The dustmen call for the rubbish once a week.* †*I'll call for you at 6.30 and we'll go out.*

call off Cancel (an arrangement, meeting, etc.) †*She gave him back his engagement ring and called off the wedding.*

call up Order (someone) to join the armed forces †*He was called up the day the war began.*

CARE *v.i.* **care for 1** Look after (a person) † *When her parents died, there was no one to care for her.* **2** Like †*I don't care for cigars unless I've eaten a good dinner beforehand.* **3** Love †*She never knew how much he cared for her.*

CARRY *v.t. & i.* **carry on** Continue or resume † *He carried on working although he was tired.* †*Carry on reading from where you left off.*

carry out Do; put into practice †*He carried out efficiently everything he was asked to do.* †*It is one thing to plan a new town, and another to carry out the plan.*

CATCH *v.t. & i.*   **catch on 1** Become popular, become the fashion †*Corduroy trousers did not catch on like jeans.* **2** Understand †*I caught on after she had explained it to me a second time.*

catch up (with) Get level with (when one has been left behind) †*Walk on ahead of me. I'll catch you up (catch up with you).*

COME *v.i.*   **come across** Find, without having looked for †*I came across this old diary in my desk.*

come off 1 Happen †*When is your visit to Paris coming off?* **2** Succeed †*I don't know if the experiment will come off, but it's worth trying.*

come out 1 Appear; become known; be published †*The stars come out at night.* †*The flowers have come out (are blooming).* †*We knew the truth would come out in the end.* †*When is your book coming out?* **2** Be resolved (mathematical) †*I've been working on this equation for an hour, but it doesn't come out.*

come round 1 Come a short distance to visit †*Come round and see me after dinner.* **2** Recur †*I always feel cheerful when Christmas comes round.* **3** Recover consciousness after fainting †*Throw some water over his face. Then perhaps he'll come round.*

COUNT *v.t. & i.*   **count on** Rely on †*You can count on him to help you.*

CUT *v.t. & i.*   **cut off 1** Break connection (on telephone) or supply (gas, electricity) †*I was talking to a friend, but the operator cut us off (we were cut off).*

DO *v.t. & i.*   **do away with** Abolish, kill †*This law is out of date. It is time the Government did away with it.* †*He has such a desperate expression that I am afraid he will do away with himself* (i.e. commit suicide).

do without Manage without †*The baker's shuts early on Wednesday, so we shall have to do without bread this evening.*

DRAW *v.t. & i.*   **draw up 1** Stop †*The car drew up outside our house.* **2** Formulate; compile (a list, plan, etc.) †*Have you drawn up a list of points for us to discuss at the meeting?*

FACE *v.t. & i.*   **face up to** Confront bravely †*You will never solve your problems unless you face up to them.*

FALL *v.i.*   **fall for** Be strongly attracted to someone or something (house, car, etc.) †*I fell for her the moment I saw her.*

fall in with Agree to †*He fell in with my suggestion without stopping to consider it.*

fall out (with) Quarrel (implying an end to relationship) †*I never expected them to fall out (with each other). They always seemed so friendly.*

fall through Come to nothing †*He applied for a number of jobs, but they all fell through.*

GET *v.t. & i.*   **get at 1** Reach †*The bottle was stuck at the back of the cupboard and I couldn't get at it.* **2** Obtain, find †*I am going to get at the truth if I have to question you for a week.* **3** Suggest, imply †*Tell me exactly what you think. I think I know what you're getting at but I want to be sure I'm right.*

get away with Avoid being punished †*He is so charming that he can insult people and get away with it!*

get down 1 Write down †*He spoke so quickly that I couldn't get it (what he said) down.* **2** Depress †*I heard that you had failed your examination, but don't let it get you down.*

get on with 1 Continue doing †*Get on with your work and don't gossip.* **2** Be on friendly terms with †*He gets on very well with everyone at work.*

get out of 1 Escape from †*The bird has got out of its cage.* †*How shall we get out of this mess?* **2** Avoid (a duty) †*You said you would help me to wash the dishes. Don't try to get out of it.*

get over (an illness, disappointment, etc.) Recover from †*I've got over the shock now, I feel much better.*

get round to Find the time to (do something, deal with someone) †*He often says he is going to write a book, but he never seems to get round to (doing) it.* †*Would you mind waiting for a moment? I'll get round to you when I have served this customer.*

GIVE *v.t. & i.*   **give up 1** Resign, abandon †*He has given up his job and retired to the country.* **2** Retire from struggle, contest †*I'm not going to give up as long as I have any chance of winning.* **3** Stop (doing something) †*I have given up smoking several times, but I always start again.*

GO *v.i.*   **go in for 1** Enter one's name for (competition, examination, etc.) †*How many of you are going in for the Proficiency examination?* **2** Take up (a sport, hobby, etc.) †*I hear you go in for stamp collecting.*

go off 1 Explode; make a loud noise †*The alarm clock went off at 7 o'clock and woke us all up.* **2** (of food, performance in game, etc.) Deteriorate; become bad †*Milk goes off very quickly in hot weather.*

go through 1 Examine carefully (of papers, plans, etc.) †*Let us go through the programme for the conference to see if we have forgotten anything.* [NOTE: The difference between this and *go over* is that here one is concentrating on the correctness of every detail, while *go over* suggests checking points already agreed, or likely to be agreed.] **2** Suffer †*She has gone through a great deal since we last met.*

go without Miss, accept the lack of †*He was so determined to finish the job that he went without his lunch.* †*I'm sorry, Peter. There are no sweets in the cupboard. You'll have to go without.*

HANG *v.t. & i.*   **hang about** Wait, without doing anything †*A group of young men were hanging about on the corner of the street.*

hang back Be unwilling to act, come forward †*We invited him to join in the game but he hung back.*

hang up Replace telephone receiver, ending call †*Don't hang up! I have something else to tell you.*

HOLD *v.t. & i.*   **hold out 1** Continue resistance; not give in †*They held out for three days before the enemy broke through their defence.* **2** Last; be enough †*Will the milk hold out until tomorrow?*

hold up Delay †*The train was held up by fog.*

KEEP *v.t. & i.*   **keep on 1** Continue †*He kept on working until he was 70 years old.* **2** Do something repeatedly †*She keeps on telling me that we should buy a new car.* **3** Not dismiss someone †*This part of the factory has been closed down, but we are keeping the men on in other jobs.*

keep up with Not fall behind †*He ought not to be in this class. He can't keep up with the rest.* †*Don't walk so fast. I can't keep up with you.*

LET *v.t. & i.* **let down** Not fulfil one's obligation (to someone) †*You can trust me to help you. I won't let you down.*

let off 1 Excuse, pardon †*The judge let him off with a warning.* †*I'll let you off your homework as it is the last week of term.* **2** Fire off (fireworks) or allow to fire (gun, etc.)

LIVE *v.i. & t.* **live on 1** Continue to live †*Her brother died in 1924 but she lived on until a few years ago.* **2** (of money, income) Spend on things one needs for living †*How much have you got to live on?* **3** Have as food †*He lives on fruit and nuts.*

live up to 1 Fulfil (promise) †*He did not live up to the great expectations everyone once had of him.* **2** Reach the standard expected of †*The hotel did not live up to its reputation.*

LOOK *v.i. & t.* **look after** Take care of †*Will you look after the children for me while I go out shopping?* †*Look after your own affairs and don't interfere in mine.*

look forward to Anticipate with pleasure †*I look forward to seeing you again.*

look into Investigate †*I'll look into your complaint, Madam, and find out who was to blame.*

look on 1 Regard, consider †*We look on this invention as one of the most important in modern times.* **2** Take no active part, be only a spectator †*I couldn't stand there looking on when I saw him attacking the girl.*

look out (usually Imperative) Take care (of yourself) †*Look out! There's a car coming towards us.*

look over 1 (house) View, to see if it is worth buying †*I must stay in tomorrow. Some people are coming to look over our house.* **2** Examine papers, letters, etc. to make sure they are all right.

look up (in a book) Find a reference †*Look up his number in the telephone book.*

look up to Respect, admire †*I have looked up to him since I was a small boy.*

MAKE *v.t. & i.* **make out 1** Write out, fill in (bill, form, etc.) †*Shall I make the cheque out in your name?* **2** (a case) Formulate or prove †*The Government is trying to make out a case for simplifying taxation.* **3** Distinguish (in seeing, reading, etc.) (usually in spite of difficulty) †*Through the fog he could just make out the shape of the church in front of him.* †*I can't make out his writing.*

make up 1 Complete, supply a deficiency †*How many stamps do you need to make up the set?* †*I can only let you have half your order now. I'll make it up next week.* **2** Invent (a story, excuse, etc.) †*He made up stories for his children.* **3** (a quarrel) Become friends, lovers again †*My husband and I have some terrible rows, but we always kiss and make up afterwards.*

make up for Compensate for †*He was too ill to go to the children's party, so we bought him a toy to make up for it.*

PAY *v.t. & i.* **pay off** Make a final payment (to someone), settle (debt, etc.) †*We hope to pay off what we owe next month.*

PICK *v.t. & i.* **pick up 1** Acquire; get to know (articles, information, languages) without conscious effort †*I picked up this copy of 'Hamlet' on a secondhand bookstall.* †*I was never taught German, but I have picked up a working knowledge of it on my visits to Germany.* **2** Increase (of trade, business, speed) †*Business has picked up now that Christmas is near* (implying that it was not good before that). †*The train picked up speed as we left the city.* **3** Improve (of health) †*She has picked up gradually since the doctor came.* **4** Call for (in a car); give a lift to †*I'll pick you up at your house at 7 o'clock.* †*We picked up two people whose car had broken down.*

PULL *v.t. & i.* **pull off** Succeed in (a plan, action) (in spite of competition, obstacles) †*The thieves have pulled off one of the most daring robberies of the century.*

pull up (of cars, trains, etc.) Stop †*He pulled up at the traffic lights.*

PUT *v.t. & i.* **put by (aside)** Save money for some future need †*He puts by five pounds a week for his summer holiday.*

put down Write down †*Put down your expenses on this form and the company accountant will give you the money.*

put in for Apply for, enter one's name for (a job, examination) †*Did you get the job you put in for?*

put off 1 Postpone †*The meeting has been put off for a week because the boss is away.* †*We shall have to put him off until a more convenient time* (postpone our meeting with him). **2** Deter, prevent from doing something †*We are not going to be put off by threats.* **3** Keep (someone) from reacting against (by excuses, lies, etc.) †*You are not going to put me off with that story.* **4** Cause (someone) to lose concentration †*His opponent's remarks put him off (his game)* †*Will it put you off if I have the television on while you're writing your letter?*

put up 1 Stay (at hotel, etc.) †*I put up for the night at the local inn.* **2** Provide accommodation for †*My brother arrived unexpectedly, so we had to put him up for the night.*

put up with Tolerate, endure (unpleasantness, inconvenience, etc.) †*I won't put up with your insults any longer.* †*People nowadays would not put up with the working conditions my father was used to* (implying that they would refuse to accept them, not that they would be too weak to stand them).

RUN *v.i. & t.* **run into** Meet (someone) by chance †*I ran into your brother in Oxford Street yesterday.*

run out 1 Expire, be due for renewal (of leases, licences, etc.) †*My television licence runs out this week.* **2** Be used up (of supplies) †*We must order some more before our stock runs out.* [ALSO: **run out of** Use up †*We have run out of butter.*]

run over 1 Read quickly or repeat main points of (article, plan, etc.) †*He ran over the main points of his speech* (either to make sure he himself was satisfied or to help the audience understand it better). **2** Knock down (in car) †*He was run over by a bus.*

SEE *v.i. & t.* **see off** Accompany (someone going on a journey) to station, airport, etc. †*We saw her off at the airport last night.*

see through Not be deceived by †*He pretended to be a rich businessman, but we saw through him (his disguise).*

see to 1 Attend to, deal with †*Will you see to this customer (letter), Miss Jones?* **2** Attend to (something) so as to ensure (that it is done) †*Everything you want will be provided. I'll see to that.* †*I'll see to it that you're not troubled any further.*

SET *v.t. & i.*   **set off 1** Start (a journey) † *The party set off (for the country) at 8 o'clock.* **2** Cause explosion of (bomb, firework, etc.) or cause (gun) to fire, (alarm) to ring †*The thief passed through the electric circuit and set off the alarm.*

set out 1 Start (a journey) (*See* **set off 1**). **2** (with **to** + infinitive) Attempt to †*He set out to prove that he was a good workman.* **3** Display (goods, etc.); present in sequence (of arguments, ideas) †*The rings were set out in the jeweller's window.* †*I have set out all the arguments in favour of the plan in my article.*

set up Establish †*The Government have set up a special department to deal with the problem.* †*When you set up house together, you will have a lot of bills to pay* (i.e. when you establish yourselves in your own house).

SIT *v.i. & t.*   **sit for** (an examination) Take.

sit up (for someone) Not go to bed (because one is waiting for him) †*We have let the children sit up to watch this programme.* †*He always sits up for his daughter.*

STAND *v.i. & t.*   **stand by 1** Support, take the side of †*Don't be afraid. I'll stand by you if you need help.* **2** Stick to (one's promise, word) †*I will stand by the agreement.* **3** Be ready (to act, move) †*The police are standing by in case the demonstration becomes violent.*

stand for 1 Represent; symbolise †*The letters UNO stand for the United Nations Organisation.* †*The stars on the flag of the United States stand for the states of the Union.* **2** Put up with, tolerate †*I won't stand for any more insults.*

stand in for Deputise for, temporarily take the place of †*I am standing in for the Chairman, who is unable to be at the meeting.*

stand out (of people) Be easily seen in relation to others, physically or mentally; (of a feature of the landscape) be easily seen in relation to its surroundings †*His painting is so good that it stands out from the rest.* †*The castle stands out on top of the hill, dominating the countryside round about.*

stand up for Defend, work for, speak in favour of †*If you are not prepared to stand up for yourself, how can we help you?*

stand up to 1 Continue to function, work (in spite of) (wear, hard usage, etc.) †*My leg is better, but I doubt if it would stand up to a lot of exercise.* †*These components are required to stand up to great pressure.* **2** Be prepared to resist attack from (someone bigger or stronger) †*Their army is much bigger than ours, but we will stand up to them.*

TAKE *v.t. & i.*   **take after** Look or act like (a parent or relation) †*You can see from his nose that he takes after his father.*

take in 1 Include †*The tour of Paris takes in a visit to the Eiffel Tower.* **2** Understand and think about †*A language teacher must speak slowly and clearly so that the students can take in everything he/she says.* **3** Deceive, trick †*I'm afraid you've been taken in. These pearls are not genuine.*

take off (of an aeroplane) Leave the ground †*Flight 123 to Paris will take off in five minutes.*

take on 1 Undertake †*I'm too busy to take on any more work.* **2** Engage (employees) †*We have taken on more staff.*

take over 1 Take control of †*When my boss retires, his son will take over the firm.* **2** Take control, responsibility (intransitive) †*When the pilot left the controls, the co-pilot took over.* †*Who will take over while you are away?*

take to 1 Start on (a course of action which continues) (particularly in set phrases 'take to crime, drink, etc.') † *She had an unhappy childhood. Her mother left home and her father took to drink* (i.e. started drinking alcohol heavily). **2** Develop a liking for †*The children have taken to their new teacher.* †*He was afraid of the sea at first, but he has taken to it since he learned to swim.*

take up 1 Occupy (time, space) †*I won't take up any more of your time.* †*That bookcase takes up a lot of room.* **2** Adopt (as a profession, business, hobby, etc.) †*He worked in an office for some years, and then took up teaching.* †*I think I will take up golf.*

THINK *v.t. & i.*

think of 1 Have an idea, conception of †*I didn't know how to mend it until I thought of putting these wires together.* **2** Recall, call to mind †*Now that I think of it, aren't you the young man who gave me a lift home last Sunday?* [ALSO. **come to think of it** Now that I recall it.] **3** Entertain as an idea †*It was an awful place. I wouldn't think of going there for a holiday.* **4** Consider the idea of; have as a half-formed intention †*We are thinking of going to live at the seaside.* **5** To indicate an opinion †*What do you think of our new wallpaper?* **6** Imagine †*Think of what would happen if the level of the Thames rose ten metres without warning.* **7** Be interested in †*She thinks of no one but herself* (i.e., she is selfish).

think out Think about until one arrives at a solution †*I have thought out the theory I told you about and I believe it will stand up to any test.*

think over Think about at length (before giving a decision, opinion) †*I can't say 'Yes' or 'No' to the plan now. I must have time to think it over.*

TRY *v.t. & i.*

try on Put on (coat, dress, shoe, etc.) to see if it fits or is suitable †*She tried on ten hats before she found one that she liked.*

try out Test (an idea, theory) in practice or (*See* **try on**) test (a machine, car, etc.) to see if it works satisfactorily, is suitable, etc. †*These exercises are quite good. Try them out in your class.* †*Before you buy the car, try it out.*

TURN *v.t. & i.*

turn down 1 Reject †*His proposals were turned down.* †*They turned him down for the job because of his age.* **2** Reduce (electric power).

turn out 1 Produce (particularly goods) †*The factory turns out 100 cars a day.* **2** Prove (to be) in the end †*The weather turned out fine.* †*We thought the party would be boring, but it turned out better than we had expected.* †*We waited for him at the station, but afterwards it turned out that he had come by car* (it became known).

turn up Arrive, appear †*I was wondering when you would turn up.* †*He is looking for a job, but so far nothing has turned up.*

WEAR *v.t. & i.*   **wear off** Gradually disappear, fade, etc. †*My tooth is aching again because the effect of the aspirin I took is wearing off.* †*The coat of paint I put on the door is wearing off.*

wear out 1 Use up, exhaust (strength, energy); make useless by wear (articles of clothing, machines, etc.) †*Looking after so many children wears me out.* †*I feel worn out* (exhausted). †*He wears out his shoes in a few weeks.* †*My clothes are worn out.* **2** Become useless through wear †*Clothes seem to wear out more quickly than they did when I was a boy.*

WORK *v.i. & t.*   **work out 1** Calculate †*Can you work the sum out in your head?* **2** Amount to, by calculation †*If we sell 20 machines for £1,000, that works-out at £50 each.* **3** Produce a result, by calculation †*This equation doesn't work out.* **4** Devise †*We have worked out a system for improving the delivery of materials.*